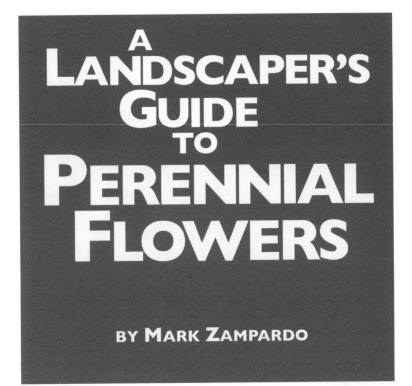

A LANDSCAPER'S GUIDE TO PERENNIAL FLOWERS

BY MARK ZAMPARDO

A
LANDSCAPER'S
GUIDE
TO
PERENNIAL
FLOWERS

BY MARK ZAMPARDO

Published by American Nurseryman Publishing Co.
223 W. Jackson Blvd., Suite 500
Chicago, IL 60606
www.amerinursery.com

Published by American Nurseryman Publishing Co.
223 W. Jackson Blvd., Suite 500
Chicago, IL 60606
www.amerinursery.com

ISBN 978-1-887632-01-0

Printed in the United States of America

Dedication

This book is dedicated to my grandfather, John Romanowski,
and my parents, Samuel and Eleanor Zampardo.
My grandfather, a long-time farmer, taught me as a young boy
how to plant and care for a garden.
My parents gave me the opportunity to experiment
in the family yard with vegetables, flowers, trees and shrubs.
Their encouragement is responsible for my education
and career in teaching for 30 years.

This watercolor was painted by my mother.

I thank them.

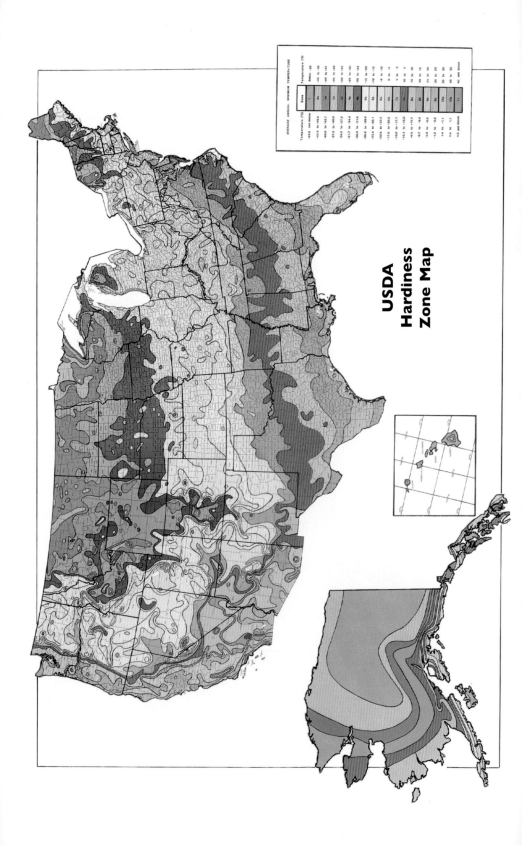

USDA
Hardiness
Zone Map

Table of Contents

Introduction

This is a plant identification book, pure and simple.

Whether you're installing flowering perennials or purchasing them, you're often presented with row upon row of plants in containers — and no blooms. If you're unfamiliar with the plants' other identifying characteristics, how do you know which to choose?

It's easy. Just follow the simple clues offered here. Designed to be used on the job site or at the garden center, this easy-to-read guide provides pertinent information on nearly 200 of the most common flowering perennials. Each page features one plant, beautifully illustrated with full-color photographs that highlight the plant's foliage and shape as well as its flower. Also included are the plant's Latin and common names, complete with a simple pronunciation guide; a brief description of the plant's key identifying characteristics; and space for the reader's own notes.

Simple, consistent descriptions and limited use of botanical terminology allow for easy reading, providing a good introduction for those new to landscaping or gardening, and those who are learning English as a second language.

An easy-to-understand guide to botanical nomenclature gives the reader a quick lesson in plant names, and a handy glossary of common botanical terms — presented in both English and Spanish — is provided as well. Glossary definitions are offered in language that is consistent, simple and easy to understand. You'll also find a convenient index of Latin and common names for quick and easy reference.

These features make *A Landscaper's Guide to Perennials* ideal for Spanish-speaking landscapers and gardeners with limited English reading skills. The guide was originally developed for use in the author's plant identification classes, which were especially designed to accommodate Spanish speakers in the landscape profession, in addition to native speakers of English.

How plants are named

The formal, botanical name of a plant is always in Latin, so sometimes it is called the Latin name. This name always has a minimum of two parts; thus, the method we use to give a plant a formal name is called the "binomial" naming system.

Family Name

Plants in the same family share characteristics such as types of flowers and fruit. The family name always ends with "aceae" (pronounced AY-see-ee). In the binomial system, the family name is not part of the formal name of the plant.

When written: The family name begins with a capital letter, but it does not appear in italics.

Examples: Asteraceae

Liliaceae

Rosaceae

Genus

Inside the family group, a more closely related group is called the genus. It is the first name in the formal name of the plant.

When written: The genus always begins with a capital letter, and it is always in italics when it is typed. (If you write the name by hand, underline it.)

Examples: *Aster*

Lilium

Rosa

Specific Epithet

The specific epithet is the second name in the formal name of the plant. It gives more information about the particular plant.

When written: The specific epithet is in lower case letters and appears in italics when it is typed. (If you write the name by hand, underline it.)

Examples: *angustifolia*

nigra

siberica

Cultivar

The cultivar name is part of the formal name for plants that have been created or selected intentionally and whose unique characteristics are maintained through cultivation. The term "cultivar" is shortened from "*CUL*tivated *VAR*iety." When there is a cultivar name, it is the third part of the formal name.

When written: The cultivar name begins with a capital letter, and it is inside single quotation marks. It does not appear in italics. (If you write the name by hand, do not underline it but use the single quotation marks.)

Examples: 'Kobold'

'Grandiflora'

'Yellow Bunting'

Variety (var.)

The variety name is also part of the formal name for plants. A variety, listed as (var.) in this book, has qualities that differ from the species but when planted from seed will have the same characteristics as the parent plant. Sometimes we cannot see the differences, such hardiness.

When written: The variety name begins with a lower case letter and is in italics when it is typed or underlined when hand-written. (The abbreviated indication "var." does not appear in italics.)

Examples: var. *alba*

              var. *atropurpurea*

              var. *glauca*

Hybrid

A hybrid is a plant that results from a cross between two or more plants that are similar. In the formal name, a hybrid is indicated by the inclusion of an "x" between the Genus and the Specific Epithet. Sometimes a hybrid is listed with the Genus and a cultivar only.

When written: The "x" does not appear in italics.

Example: *Gaillardia* x *grandiflora*

              Geranium x *cantabrigiense*

              Hosta 'Big Daddy'

Species

The entire formal name of the plant is called the species name.

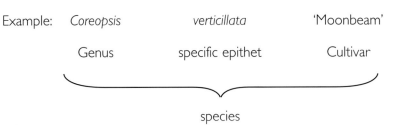

Example: *Coreopsis*   *verticillata*   'Moonbeam'

　　　　　　　Genus   specific epithet   Cultivar

　　　　　　　　　　　　　　　　　species

Common Names

The common name is the English name for the plant. It often describes the flowers, leaves, origin, medicinal properties or the discoverer. Unfortunately, some plants have several common names or the same common name is used for more than one plant. Sometimes the common name is the same as the Genus of the plant, such as *Iris* or *Coreopsis*.

Glossary
Glosary

alternate
a way the leaves grow on the stem. In alternate arrangement, two leaves are not across from each other; one grows on one side and then a little higher up the stem, another grows on the other side.
alternadas
es de la manera en que las hojas crecen a lo largo de el tallo de la planta, donde una hoja crece en un lado de el tallo y la otra crece en el otro lado pero mas arriba.

base (leaf)
part of the leaf nearest to the stem
base (foliar)
parte de la hoja que esta mas cerca del tallo

bearded
having long hairs
ligulado
barbado; caracteristica tipica del iris barbado

berm
small or narrow hill or mound that is made for good drainage or protection
loma
pequeña y angosta loma hecha para mejorar el drenaje

blade (leaf)
part of the leaf from the base to the tip
lamina foliar
lamina de la hoja con el tallo

biennial
a plant that lives two years, then dies
biannual
planta que produce hojas en el primer ano de vida; flores, frutos y semillas en el segundo y despues muere

bi-pinnate
pinnate two times; in other words, the main stem of the leaf divides into two groups of leaflets
bi-pinada
es cuando el tallo de la hoja principal se divide en dos grupos de hojuelas

14

bloom
a flower coming out or opening on the plant. The **bloom** time is the time that the flower is **blooming** on the plant. Another meaning is the noun: a flower
florecer, floreciendo
es una flor saliendo o abriendo en la planta. Es cuando las plantas están floreando.

bluish
blue-like color; or a color that has a little blue mixed with another color
azuloso
color azul mezclado con otro color más importante

border
the place where two different areas meet; the edge or line that divides two areas. A border flower or garden bed is next to a building or a fence.
borde
orilla, ribetear

borer
an insect that harms plants by eating inside the branches and stems. The plant or branches thus cannot get food and water, so these branches or plants die.
barrenador
es un insecto que hace agujeros en el tallo de la planta penetrando hasta el centro del mismo por lo que la planta no puede llevar agua ni nutrientes a todas sus partes y muere.

bract
flower part that looks like a petal but is actually a type of leaf
bractea
hoja modificada de la planta, que se ceirtas inflorescencias

broadleaf evergreen
kind of evergreen leaf that is relatively (more or less) broad or wide, and not awl-like, not needle-like and not scale-like
hoja ancha
son las hojas de los árboles que son anchas, no como las de los pinos que son como agujas.

bronze
brown-gold color. Another meaning is the verb: to change to a bronze color.
bronce
de color café dorado

brownish
brown-like color or color that has a little brown mixed with another color
café pardo
es la combinación de el color café con otro color mas importante

bud

beginning of a flower or leaf, before it blooms or comes out, when the flower or leaf is rolled or folded tightly

botón

parte de la planta de donde brotan las hojas y las flores

bulb

fleshy underground stem

bulbo

tallo modificado subterraneo que forma el platillo basal

capsule

dry, hard fruit

capsula

fruta seca y dura

clinging vine

a plant that can grow up on another thing (for example, a building) because it has small root parts that adhere to the other thing. It attaches to a wall or tree trunk and does not need other support.

vid trepadora

plantas con la capacidad de crecer hacia arriba sobre otras superficies ya que se adhieren a ellas con unas pequeñas raíces

cluster

grouped together; for example, a cluster of flowers is many flowers on the same stem

racimo

ramillete

columnar

like a column; a tall, narrow shape

de forma de columna

parecido a una columna, alta y angosta

compacted/compaction

pushed close together, so that there is not much air or room for water to move through easily. When soil is compacted, there is compaction in the soil.

compactado-compactación

es cuando el suelo se aprieta y no tiene aire o espacio para el agua

compound

leaf with multiple parts. There are two main kinds of compound leaves: palmate compound and pinnate compound.

compuestas

es una hoja que tiene el botón en el tallo principal con hojuelas saliendo del final de el tallo de la hoja. Hay dos formas principales de hojas compuestas: hojas palmadas y hojas pinadas.

concave
bowl shape; wide and shallow U shape
concavo
superficie en forma de plato, no pareja. Es una forma de U ancha y no muy profunda

cone/conical
something that is rounded at the wide end and has a point at the narrow end. Conical is a cone shape. Another meaning: a cone is the fruit of a conifer. It has seeds in it.
cónico
en forma de cono. Es redondo en la parte ancha y termina en punta. Otro significado para cono es el fruto de las confieras.

cultivar
a cultivated variety; one kind of a plant with some changes (for example, changes in hardiness, color, or resistance to disease or pests) that was selected by someone for the specific purpose of the change. Many cultivars belong to a specific nursery or company and so have a trademark.
cultivar
variedad de una planta que ha sido cambiada o mejorada, por ejemplo para climas, en color, tamaño, resistencia a enfermedades. Muchos cultivares pertenecen a una especifica norseria y por eso llevan su nombre.

curled
twisted or curved around and around, like a screw
ondulado
torcido o curveado a la vuelta y vuelta como tornillo

cutleaf
leaf shape with deep cuts in it
hoja cortada
hojas con cortadas profundas. El margen no es parejo.

dark
with only a little light or with more black than white in something. When we see dark before a color word (for example, dark green or dark red), it means the color has more black in it than others of the color has.
obscuro
sin mucha luz o con mas negro que blanco en algo. Cuando vemos la palabra obscuro después de otro color significa que el color tiene mas negro que el color solo.

dense
close together; thick
denso
espeso, muy junto, muy tupido

diameter

line across the middle of a circle that crosses the center of the circle. We can use the diameter to measure the size of the circle.

diámetro

línea trazada por el medio de un circulo. Podemos usar el diámetro para medir la circunferencia.

distinguish

find, see or be a difference between two or more things in one or more ways

distinguir

Es algo que marca la diferencia entre dos o mas cosas en una o mas formas

domed

half rounded, hill shape

como bóveda

es cuando algo tiene forma plana en la parte de abajo y redonda la parte de arriba. En forma de loma.

down/downy

very many thin, soft hairs or threads. Something that is downy has a lot of down on it.

esponjoso

superficie cubierta de pelo suave. Como algodón.

drainage

the way or how fast water moves through the soil. When water moves through the soil easily and quickly, the drainage is good; when the water stays in the soil for some time, the drainage is poor.

drenaje

es la manera de cómo se mueve el agua a través del suelo. Cuando se mueve muy rápido se dice que tiene buen drenaje. Cuando el agua se queda estancada hay mal drenaje.

droop/drooping

hanging or bending down

inclinarse

marchitarse

drought

a long time when there is not much water, or when the soil is dry for a long time because not much water comes into it

sequía

periodo largo de tiempo cuando escasea el agua

dwarf

kind that is smaller than another, similar, variety

enano

clase de planta mas pequeña que otra similar y de la misma variedad.

edible
okay to eat
comestible
ok a la ate

elliptic/elliptical
shape that looks like a circle, but has two sides that are flatter and longer than the others. An egg shape is an elliptical shape. An oval is another way to describe this shape.
elíptico
horma de circulo con un lado plano y el otro lado mas largo

entire
leaf shape where the edges, or margins, of the leaf don't have any teeth or cuts into them; they are smooth
entero
es cuando la orilla de la hoja o margen es completamente lisa o que no tiene dientes o cortadas.

erosion
the way the soil is removed a little at a time because of water, wind or gravity
erosión
es la forma en que el suelo es arrastrado poco a poco debido al agua, el viento, y la gravedad

erosion control
a way to stop, prevent or slow down the amount of erosion in an area; for example, by planting something so the roots will hold the soil
control de erosión
es la manera de prevenir o parar la erosión en un area; por ejemplo plantando plantas para que las raíces detengan la tierra

evergreen
kind of plant where the majority of leaves don't fall off the stems in the fall; most leaves stay on the plant all year
siempre verde
en estas plantas la mayoría de las hojas no se caen de sus ramas en el otoño; la mayoría de las hojas permanecen en la planta todo el ano

facer
plant in front of other plants, usually at the edge of a bed. These plants are usually at the front of a border or bed.
al frente
plantas colocadas enfrente de otras plantas, usualmente a la orilla de la cama

fair

okay; not very good, not bad

regular

no muy bueno, pero tampoco muy malo. Así, así.

fine

thin and/or small

fino

delgado o pequeño

foliage

leaves

follaje

area foliar de las plantas

foundation (plant)

plant we can place or use near the walls of a building. These plants are usually up against or near a house.

planta para la fundación (cimiento)

plantas que podemos usar cerca de las paredes de los edificios

fragrant

having an odor or smell, good or bad

fragante

tener buen o mal olor

full sun

six or more hours of sun shines directly on the place each day

sol todo el día

lugar con por lo menos seis horas de sol al día

fungus

very simple kind of plant without leaves or seeds or chlorophyll (the part that makes plants green) that often grows on other plants and so might harm those plants. A mushroom is an example of a fungus.

hongos

plantas simples sin hojas ni semillas y carecen de clorofila (parte que hace verdes a las plantas). Por lo general los hongos crecen en otras plantas y pueden dañarlas o hacer que las plantas se vean feas.

fuzz/fuzzy

a cover of many very thin, soft hairs. Something that is fuzzy has a lot of fuzz on it.

peludo

cubierta de pelos muy delgados y finos

gall
disease where part of the plant gets larger or swollen
yaga o bola
enfermedad donde la parte de la planta se hace larga o hinchada. Algunos insectos también pueden causar el mismo problema en la planta.

gland
part of the plant that makes a liquid; it often sticks out a little from the base of the leaf
glándula
parte de la planta que produce un liquido. Casi siempre sobresale de la base de la hoja.

glossy
shiny; leaves that are glossy are shiny leaves
glossier
brilliante, lustroso

gray or grey
color that is a combination of black and white
gris
color que resulta de combinar el blanco y el negro

greenish
green-like color; or color that has a little green mixed with another color
verdoso
es un color que tiene un poquito de color verde

groundcover
a plant that grows low to the ground and spreads thickly, so it covers the ground. These plants are usually less than 24 inches high.
cubre el suelo
plantas que crecen cerca de la superficie de la tierra y se extienden espesamente cubriendo la tierra

group
a small number of the same plant planted together in the same area
grupo
de la misma planta plantadas juntas en la misma área

habit
shape of a plant
habito
porte do una planta

hairlike
like hair; very thin
forma de cabello
muy delgado como cabello

hardy
able to stay alive in cold conditions; for example, a plant that is hardy to zone 5 can live in the temperatures of −20 degrees Fahrenheit.
resistente
capaz de vivir en ciertas condiciones; por ejemplo, una planta resistente a la zona 5 puede vivir en las temperaturas invernales de esta área.

height
how high or tall something is
altura
que tan alto esta algo

holdfasts
stem-like structure with sticky pads used by the plant to attach to (hold on to) something
ventosas
son como almohadillas pegajosas que salen del tallo de las plantas las cuales le ayudan a adherirse a algo

horizontal
kind of line that goes across, not up and down; the kind of line in the same direction as the line of the sky meeting the land or water, the horizon
horizontal
es una línea recta acostada. No va ni para arriba ni para abajo. Es la clase de línea en la misma dirección que la línea del cielo topando la tierra o el agua, el horizonte.

husk
outside cover of a seed or fruit
cáscara
es la capa que cubre a la semilla o fruto

hybrid
plant made from the mix of two or more plants
híbrido
planta hecha de la mezcla de dos o más plantas

irregular
not regular; not the same shape and/or not smooth on all sides
irregular
no regular, no la misma forma, no lisa en todos los lados

lanceolate
leaf shape where the leaf is long and narrow and the top has a sharp point or tip. It is thinner than an ovate shape.
lanceolado
en forma de lanza o lanceta, engrosado en la base y disminuyendo gradualmente hasta terminar en punta

lateral
on the side, not the end
lateral
al lado

lateral bud
side buds as opposed to the terminal bud (end bud)
yema lateral
yema que emerge de los nudos localizados debajo de la yema terminal

leaflet
small leaf parts of a compound leaf
hojitas, hojuelas
hojas pequeñas que componen una hoja compuesta

light
amount of sun a plant needs. (When we use it in this way it often appears in the phrase "light requirements.")
OR with more white than black in something. When we see the word "light" before a color word (for example, light green or light blue), it means the color has more white in it and is paler than others of the color.
bajito
con mas blanco que negro. Cuando vemos la palabra bajito después de un color significa que este color es mas claro que el color solo.

lilac
light purple color
lila
color morado claro o bajito

lobed/lobe
leaf shape that is divided into rounded parts almost to the middle. A lobe is one part of that kind of leaf. It is often rounded at the edges.
lobulo/lobuladas
tipo de hojas divididas en partes redondas casi hasta la mitad. El lóbulo es una parte de esta hoja y puede ser redondo o puntiagudo. Lóbulos son mas grandes que los dientes.

margin
edge of a leaf
margen
orilla de la hoja

maroon
dark, brown-red color
marrón
color rojo obscuro

mass
a large number of the same kind of plants (for example, 10 or 20) planted together
masas
un numero grande de plantas de la misma clase, 10 o 20 plantadas juntas

mess/messy
something not in order, not neat. A messy plant looks like a mess.
desordenado
algo que no esta ordenado, que no se ve bien.

mid
middle, not beginning or end. For example, a plant that blooms mid-April blooms near April 15.
mediado
a la mitad, no al principio o al final. Por ejemplo una planta que florea a mediados de Abril, florea cerca del 15 de Abril.

mildew (powdery mildew)
disease caused by a fungus that puts a gray powder on the leaves
enmohecido
enfermedad causada por hongos y pone polvo gris sobre las hojas

moist (moisture)
a little wet; has a little water in it
húmedo
poco mojado, tiene poco agua en el

mottled
way to describe a leaf, branch or flower where light or dark kinds of the same color appear together with no regular pattern
moteado
forma de describir cuando una hoja, rama, o flor tiene como manchas obscuras o claras del mismo color pero de diferente forma

mound (mounded)
shape like a small hill or very small mountain; like a mound
loma
forma de loma o bola, o como montana pequeña

multiple
many; more than two
multiple
muchos

naked
with nothing covering or on top of it. A naked bud has no bud scales; a naked person has no clothes.
desnudo
sin nada que lo cubra, sin protección. Un botón desnudo no tiene escamas.

narrow
thin; a small distance from one side to the other side; opposite of wide
estrecho
delgado; es la distancia pequeña entre un lado y otro. Es lo opuesto de ancho.

native
original to an area
nativa
planta originaria de la zona en donde vive

natural/naturalize/naturalizing
from nature. A natural or naturalized area is one that has plants or is planted in a way that makes it look like it is from nature.
natural/naturalizar
natural, de la naturaleza, bosques naturales

needle or needle-like
leaf shape that is very thin and straight, longer than it is wide. We can find them on many conifers.
forma de aguja
forma de hoja muy delgada y derecha, es mas larga que ancha. Se encuentran en las confieras.

node
place on a stem from which a bud, a leaf and/or a spine can grow
nudo
es la parte del tallo donde el botón, la hoja o una espina se desarrollan

oblong
leaf shape that has similar widths at the top and the bottom of the leaf so it looks rectangular, but with more rounded edges
oblongo
dar forma huevo

onion skin
bark that peels, or comes off the stem, one thin layer at one time. We can take off this thin layer very easily, with the fingernail.
piel de cebolla
es cuando la cáscara del tallo se pela en capas delgadas una por una y pueden ser removidas con las unas o dedos.

opposite
a way leaves grow on the stem where two leaves and buds grow across from each other
opuesto
es la forma en que las hojas crecen en el tallo donde dos hojas y botones crecen cruzados uno del otro

oval
shape that looks like an egg; like a circle that is longer at the ends than in the middle; elliptic
ovalado
forma de huevo como un circulo que es mas largo en las puntas que a la mitad

palmate compound
a way leaflets are connected to the main leaf stem of a compound leaf where each leaflet meets at a single point, like the fingers meet in the palm of the hand
palmada compuesta
es la manera en que las hojas están conectadas al tallo principal de la hoja donde se conectan a un solo punto como los dedos a la palma de la mano

panicle
kind of flower where small flowers grow on small parts that look like stems
panicula
tipo de flores donde pequeñas flores crecen en pequeñas partes que parecen tallos

part shade
no more than a few hours of sun that is non-direct or appears through leaves (dappled)
parte de sombra
pocas horas de sol. Que no pegue directamente o que pase a través de las hojas. Hay mas sol que sombra.

part sun
three to five hours of sun shines directly on the place each day
parte de sol
tres a cinco horas de sol pegando directamente en un lugar diariamente. Hay mas sombra que sol.

persist/persistent
stay on the plant even after death. Something that is persistent stays on the plant even after it dies.
persistente
permanece en la planta aun después de que se muere

pest
plant or animal that hurts another plant (insects and diseases)
plaga
planta o animal que daña a otra planta

petiole

stem-like part of a leaf; part that attaches to the stem

pecíolo

es la parte de la hoja que se adhiere al tallo

pH

a way to measure the amount of acid in the soil. When the soil has more acid, there is a lower number: 7 means the soil is neutral. When the soil has a higher number, it has less acid and is alkaline.

pH

es la manera de medir la acidez o alcalinidad del suelo. Mas ácido significa un numero mas pequeño. El numero 7 esta a la mitad y significa que el suelo es neutro.

pinnate (pinnate compound)

a way leaflets are connected to the main leaf stem of a compound leaf

pinada compuesta

es la forma en que las hojuelas están conectadas al tallo principal de la hoja compuesta donde cada hojuela no se toca una con otra

pith

soft material in the middle of stems and branches

medula

tejido suave y esponjoso del centro do los tallos y ramas de las plantas monocotiledoneas

pod

kind of fruit where the cover of the seeds is dry and divides easily into two halves, like a pea

vaina

es el tipo de fruta donde la cubierta de la semillas se seca y se divide en dos mitades muy fácilmente, como el frijol

pome

kind of fruit with a lot of thick material inside it; for example, an apple or a pear

pomo

ee le llama así al tipo de fruto como la manzana y la pera

powdery mildew

see mildew. Powdery mildew is another name for the same disease.

mildiu polvorento

enfermedad causada principalmente por hongos de los generos

prickle
kind of changed (modified) bark that looks like a little spine and is sharp at the tip, but is easy to take off. Prickles can grow at the end of leaves or on the stem.
espinas
corteza modificada que parece espinas y son picudas pero fácil de remover. Pueden crecer en hojas o tallos.

prune
remove parts of a plant to improve its health, appearance and/or shape
podar
acción de cortar o remover parte de las plantas para que se vea y crezca mejor

pubescent
having short, soft hairs
pubescente
que tiene como bellos cortos y suaves

purplish
purple-like color or color with some purple mixed with some other color
moradizo
es el color morado mezclado con otro

pyramidal
like a pyramid (a building in a triangle shape)
pyramidal
tiene forma de pirámide o de triangulo

raceme
kind of flower/fruit clusters. These clusters look like a little spike.
racimo
tipo de flor o fruto que se agrupan y crecen como espiga

ragged
not even, not good looking
irregular
que no se ve bien, no es pareja

reddish
red-like color or color where red is mixed with another color
rojizo
color rojo mezclado con otro

rhizome
stem that grows under the ground
rizoma
tallos que crecen debajo de la tierra

ridge
long, narrow part that is higher than other parts around it
cresta
es como un bordo o protuberancia a lo largo del tallo

rootlet
small and like a root
raicilla
una arraigar pequena

roundish
a little round in shape
redondeada
con forma redonda

rust
red-brown color; the color iron becomes after it stays wet for a while. Another meaning: the name of a leaf disease. In this disease the leaf has rust-colored spots on the top of the leaf and threads on the underside.
moho
color café rojizo que aparece después de haber estado mojado por un tiempo. Rust es el nombre de una enfermedad de las hojas. En esta enfermedad la hoja tiene manchas de color rojizo por arriba y por debajo de la hoja tiene como hebras o hilos pequeños.

scale or scale-like
an insect and the disease the insect causes on a plant. In spring the insect has a soft body and crawls; pesticides can kill the insects at this time. In summer the insect lives under a hard shell and later makes a sticky egg mass. On some conifers the leaves look like the skin (scales) of a fish where small parts of the leaf are on top of each other. Another meaning is a part of some buds. Buds can also have scales, or thin parts on top of the bud.
escamas
enfermedad causada por un insecto en la planta; en la primavera el insecto tiene un cuerpo suave y gatea; los pesticidas pueden matarlo en este tiempo. En el verano vive en una concha dura y es cuando pone sus huevos. Hojas que parecen piel de pescado donde las pequeñas partes de la hoja crecen una arriba de la otra. Las encontramos en muchas confieras. Los botones también pueden tener escamas.

screen
a row of shrubs that covers an area completely, so nobody can see through it. It blocks something we don't usually want to see.
barrera, pantalla
linea de arbustos que cubre un área completamente para que nadie pueda ver

serrate
leaf shape with a toothed edge, with the teeth pointing forward, like the teeth of a saw
serrada
tipo de hoja como con dientes de serrucho que apuntan para afuera

sessile
leaf attached to a stem without a petiole
sesil
flor sin pedunculo, que descansa directamente en el tallo

shade
a place that has no sun shining directly on it, so it is darker than a place with sun
sombra
el sol no ilumina directamente el lugar por lo que esta más obscuro que un lugar soleado

shaggy
looking like messy hair, rough and growing on top of another; not smooth or neat
entreverado
parece pelo sin peinar, enredado, embaranado creciendo uno arriba de otro. No suave, no bonito.

shallow
not deep; close to the top of the soil
encima
no muy profundo

shear
cut with a tool like a large scissors
cortar parejo
cortar con tijeras muy largas

shine/shiny
looks bright and shows a lot of light. Something that is shiny is bright and shines a lot.
brilloso
algo luminoso que refleja la luz

shoot
newly growing branch or leaf
vastago
desarrollo de nuevos brotes de las plantas, por lo gereral en las axilas de las hojas

simple
leaf type with a blade and petiole only
sencilla
hoja donde el boton de la misma esta en el tallo principal de la hoja.

single
one by itself
solo
que se encuentra solo sin otros mas

sinus
area between the lobes or parts of a leaf
seno
es el área entre los lóbulos de la oreja

slope
ground higher at one end than another (for example, when there is a hill, so water moves down in that direction). Another meaning is the verb: to have a slope. For example, a hill can slope down to a lake.
inclinación
cuando el nivel del suelo es mas alto en un lado que en otro

specimen
one plant that grows alone in a place where it is easy to see and is the most important plant in the area
ejemplar
planta que crece sola en un lugar donde es fácil de ver y es la más importante en el área

spice/spicy
odor or smell or taste that is sharp and sweet, like cinnamon or cardamom. The adjective is spicy, meaning "with spice."
especial
aroma que huele o sabe picoso como canela

spider mite
pest with eight legs and two major parts in its body, like a very small spider
arana/acaro
plaga parecida a las arañas, tiene ocho patas y dos partes del cuerpo

spike
tall, narrow, strong stem that flowers grow on, usually without branches
espiga
tallo alto y delgado donde las flores crecen usualmente sin ramas

spine/spiny
a piece coming out from the stem that is straight, strong and sharp at the end. Spines are changed leaves. They are green in the summer and brown in the winter. Spiny means many spines.
espina
protuberancias puntiagudas y fuertes que nacen del tallo de la planta. Son hojas modificadas. Son verdes en el verano y cafés en el invierno.

spread
width; how wide something is. Another meaning is the verb: to move out or grow out and cover an area.
extiende
anchura; que tan ancho es algo. Verbo: moverse o crecer para afuera y cubrir un área.

spur
a short, straight branch on which flowers and fruit grow in some trees
espuela
son ramas que crecen del tallo o tronco principal de la planta, es corto, con las flores y frutos creciendo de ellas. Las manzanas crecen en espuelas.

stipule
a thick part of leaf next to the petiole (at the base of the leaf). Sometimes the stipule looks like an ear.
estipula
estructura en forma de hoja que nace en la base del peciolo de algunas plantas

stolon
a stem that grows along the ground, horizontally
estolón
tallos que crecen horizontalmente en la superficie de la tierra

subopposite
a way the leaves grow on the stem where two leaves are almost opposite, almost across from each other
subopuesto
forma de crecer de las hojas en el tallo casi opuestas

sucker
a new stem that grows up from the root or from under the soil
retoño
brotes o ramas nuevas que crecen de la raíz

tapered
a shape that gradually becomes narrower until it reaches a point at the end
estrechar
algo que es ancho y termina largo y angosto

terminal
at the end or tip of a stem or branch
terminal
es donde termina el tallo o rama

thin

very narrow, opposite of wide; skinny. Another meaning is to make a plant thinner by cutting some branches or stems.

delgado

muy angosto, opuesto de ancho. Flaco. Verbo: Hacer la planta delgada cortándola ramas.

thorn

a kind of twig or branch that grows from the stem that is straight, strong and sharp at the end. Thorns are a changed (modified) kind of stem or branch.

espinas

protuberancias derechas, duras, y puntiagudas que crecen del tallo de la planta. Son ramas o tallos modificados, son cafes todo el ano.

till

use tools to dig into the soil

cultivar

es el uso de herramientas para escarbar en el suelo

tip

corner or end of something, usually with a sharper or pointed shape, like the end of a triangle

punta

esquina o fin de algo que es puntiagudo como el final de un triangulo

tolerant

able to live even when conditions are difficult; for example, when the plant is salt-tolerant, it can continue to grow even when there is some salt near it or in its soil.

tolerante

capaz de vivir en condiciones difíciles; por ejemplo plantas tolerantes a la sal

toothed

leaf shape that has edges (margins) that are not smooth and appear cut into small pieces, like sharp teeth

dentado

hoja con margen con dientes, no es liso

transplant

move a plant from one place to another place

transplantar

acción de mover una planta de un lugar a otro

trellis

a frame for climbing plants to grow up on

espaldera

escalera para plantas

trifoliate
having three leaflets
trifoliada
hoja con tres hojuelas

underside
the bottom of the leaf; the part of the leaf we don't usually see from the top
en el lado de abajo
parte de debajo de la hoja, no la vemos

upright
standing straight up
parado
que crece derecho hacia arriba

variety
one kind of the same plant with some changes; for example, changes in hardiness or color. In the Latin name, the variety is last.
variedad
clase de planta de la misma especie con algunos cambios por ejemplo en resistencia o color. En el nombre latín la variedad esta al ultimo.

variegated
more than one color; for example green and white leaves
multicolor
con mas de un color

vary
change in one or more ways; be different or changing
varia
cambia de una o mas maneras

vein
very thin line or tube in a stem or leaf that carries food to parts of the plant
vena
tubos delgados dentro de la hoja o el tallo que acarrean comida a las partes de la planta

violet
color that is a little lighter than purple
violeta
color mas claro que el morado

wavy
like a wave; not straight but moving down in little half round shapes
ondulado
como ondas, no derecho, que se mueve hacia abajo en formas medio redondas

weeping
branches grow down or droop
colgante
ramas creciendo hacia abajo

whitish
a color with some white in it, or is close to a white color
blancuzco
color casi blanco

whorled
a way the leaves grow from the stem where three or more leaves grow from the same place of the stem
espiral
forma en que las hojas crecen en el tallo y mas de tres crecen en el mismo lugar

width
how wide something is; the distance from one side to another side
anchura
lo ancho de algo o la distancia de un lado a otro

wing/winged
seed with a part like the wing of a bird. It is often dry and thin. With wings: A winged seed.
ala/alado
semilla que vuela con alas

wine
red-purple color
vino
color vino, rojo morado

winterburn
leaves turning brown or dying because the winter wind dries them too much
helada
hojas que se hacen cafés o mueren debido a que el viento del invierno las reseca

yellowish
has a little yellow color mixed with another, more dominant color
amarillento
es un color con poco amarillo en el

x
the symbol that indicates a plant is a hybrid. In a Latin or binomial name, X shows the plant is a hybrid.
x
en el nombre latín representa a una planta híbrida

Achillea filipendulina

Achillea filipendulina
(ak-ih-LEE-uh fil-ih-PEN-dyoo-LY-nuh)

Common Name	Fern-Leafed Yarrow
Leaves	Deep cut, feather-like, spicy odor when crushed, dull green
Flowers	Yellow, flat cluster 3-4 inches across
Bloom Time	Late spring to mid summer, 4-6 weeks
Size/Shape	3-4 feet high and wide, round clump
Special Requirements	Full sun, dry soil, low maintenance
Garden Use	Border, mass
Hardiness Zone	3-8
Other Notes	A. x 'Moonshine' is a hybrid with yellow flowers and a shorter habit
Your Own Notes	_____
	_____
	_____

Achillea millefolium

Achillea millefolium
(ak-ih-LEE-uh mil-ih-FO-lee-um)

Common Name	Common Yarrow
Leaves	Alternate, simple, deeply cut, fern-like, fragrant when crushed
Flowers	White, red to pink cultivars, flat terminal clusters
Bloom Time	Mid to late summer
Size/Shape	1-2 feet tall, 2-3 feet wide, spreads by rhizomes
Special Requirements	Full sun and good drainage, spreads fast, divide every 2 years
Garden Use	Perennial border, cut flowers, mass
Hardiness Zone	4-8
Other Notes	The species is a common weed with white flowers. The cultivars and hybrids have colorful flowers (pictures above)
Your Own Notes	_____
	_____
	_____

Aconitum napellus
(ak-o-NY-tum nuh-PEL-us)

Common Name	Monkshood
Leaves	Alternate, deep cut leaves
Flowers	Blue or violet, spike-like racemes, each flower shaped like a hood or helmet
Bloom Time	Mid to late summer
Size/Shape	3-4 feet tall, 1 to 1½ feet wide
Special Requirements	Part shade, keep soil moist, cut back after flowering for more flowers
Garden Use	Mixed border
Hardiness Zone	3-7
Other Notes	Poisonous if eaten, avoid skin contact
Your Own Notes	_____

Aegopodium podagraria 'Variegatum'

Aegopodium podagraria 'Variegatum'
(ee-go-PO-dee-um po-duh-GRAYR-ee-uh vayr-ee-GAY-tum)

Common Name Bishop's Weed
Leaves Compound leaves, with white margins
Flowers White, not showy
Bloom time May-June
Size/Shape 8-10 inches tall, spreading groundcover
Special Requirements Sun or shade, any soil, prune out solid green leaves
Garden Use Groundcover
Hardiness Zone 4-8
Other Notes Difficult to kill, may be aggressive. The species has green leaves (pictured lower right)
Your Own Notes _____
_____
_____

Agastache foeniculum

Agastache foeniculum
(uh-GAS-tuh-kee; a-guh-STAY-kee; a-guh-STAH-kee fee-NIK-yoo-lum)

Common Name	Giant Hyssop; Anise Hyssop
Leaves	Opposite, ovate, serrate, anise odor when crushed, square stems
Flowers	Lavender to purple, 4-5 inch spikes
Bloom time	Late summer
Size/Shape	3 feet tall, 3 feet wide
Special Requirements	Full sun, good drainage
Garden Use	Borders, butterfly garden, herb garden
Hardiness Zone	5-9
Other Notes	Flowers can be dried, leaves used in potpourris and in tea
Your Own Notes	_____
	_____
	_____

Ajuga reptans

Ajuga reptans
(AJ-yoo-guh; a-JYOO-guh REP-tanz)

Common Name Ajuga or Bugleweed
Leaves Leaves attached at the crown (basal), shiny, wrinkled
Flowers Violet spikes, square stems
Bloom Time Early spring
Size/Shape 6-9 inches tall, groundcover, spreads by runners
Special Requirements Sun to shade, any soil, except wet
Garden Use Groundcover for shade, where grass does not grow
Hardiness Zone 4-8
Other Notes Many cultivars with different colored leaves
Your Own Notes _____
_____
_____

Alcea rosea
(al-SEE-uh; AL-see-uh RO-zee-uh)

Common Name	Hollyhock
Leaves	Alternate, 3 to 5 lobes, rough
Flowers	Many colors; white, pink, red, yellow, lavender on tall spikes
Bloom Time	Midsummer to fall
Size/Shape	2 to 9 feet tall
Special Requirements	Full sun, good drainage, Japanese beetles eat the leaves
Garden Use	Background, against a fence or wall
Hardiness Zone	3-7
Other Notes	Biennial, self seeds
Your Own Notes	_____
	_____
	_____

Alchemilla mollis

Alchemilla mollis
(al-keh-MIL-uh MOL-liss)

Common Name	Lady's Mantle
Leaves	Round leaves with small lobes, silky hairs (pubescent)
Flowers	Yellow to light green
Bloom Time	Late spring to early summer
Size/Shape	18-20 inches tall, clump forming
Special Requirements	Full sun to part shade, moist soil
Garden Use	Front of border, in groups or use as a groundcover
Hardiness Zone	4-7
Other Notes	
Your Own Notes	_____

_____

_____

Allium giganteum

Allium giganteum
(AL-ee-um jy-gan-TEE-um; jih-GAN-tee-um)

Common Name	Giant Allium
Leaves	18 inches long, 2 inches wide, strap-like, smell like onions when crushed
Flowers	Lilac-pink, small, star-shaped, in round clusters 4-5 inches wide, on a long stem, 3-4 feet tall
Bloom Time	Late spring
Size/Shape	Leaves 18 inches tall, flower stem 3-4 feet tall, 2 feet wide
Special Requirements	Full sun to part shade, good drainage, plant bulbs in the fall
Garden Use	Perennial border in groups
Hardiness Zone	5-8
Other Notes	Leaves die back after flowering
Your Own Notes	_____
	_____
	_____

Allium sphaerocephalon

Allium sphaerocephalon
(AL-ee-um sfeer-o-SEF-uh-lon)

Common Name	Drumstick Chives
Leaves	3-5 leaves per plant, hollow tubes, fragrant like onions
Flowers	Reddish purple, round cluster of flowers
Bloom Time	Midsummer bloom
Size/Shape	2-3 feet tall
Special Requirements	Full sun, good drainage
Garden Use	Plant in groups, good cut flower
Hardiness Zone	4-8
Other Notes	Bulb
Your Own Notes	_____
	_____
	_____

Amsonia tabernaemontana

Amsonia tabernaemontana
(am-SO-nee-uh tuh-bur-nee-mon-TAY-nuh)

Common Name	Blue Star
Leaves	Alternate, narrow, sessile to the stem, good yellow fall color
Flowers	Blue, star shaped, in clusters at terminals
Bloom Time	Early summer
Size/Shape	2-3 feet tall, 3 feet wide
Special Requirements	Full sun to part shade, moist soil
	Needs staking in the shade
Garden Use	Group or mass in borders
Hardiness Zone	3-9
Other Notes	*Amsonia hubrictii* has lighter blue flowers and yellow fall color and is less common (pictured lower left)
Your Own Notes	_____
	_____
	_____

Anchusa azurea

Anchusa azurea
(an-KYOO-sah a-ZYOO-ree-uh)

Common Name	Italian Bugloss
Leaves	Alternate, rough hairy leaves, winged petiole
Flowers	Blue, loose racemes
Bloom Time	Late spring
Size/Shape	3-5 feet tall, floppy
Special Requirements	Full sun to part shade, good drainage
Garden Use	Groups, mass, border
Hardiness Zone	3-8
Other Notes	Nice blue flowers, short lived
Your Own Notes	_____
	_____
	_____

Anemone x *hybrida*

Anemone x **hybrida**
(uh-NEM-o-nee HY-brih-duh)

Common Name	Japanese Anemone
Leaves	Long petioles with 3 leaflets, lobed margins
Flowers	White or pink flowers at top of plant, yellow eye
Bloom Time	Late summer into fall
Size/Shape	2-3 feet tall, spread by rhizomes
Special Requirements	Full sun to part shade, good drainage, moist soils
Garden Use	Border, woodlands
Hardiness Zone	4-8
Other Notes	Cultivars available with pink flowers and double flowers
Your Own Notes	_____
	_____
	_____

Anemone sylvestris

Anemone sylvestris
(uh-NEM-o-nee sil-VESS-triss)

Common Name	Snowdrop Anemone
Leaves	Simple, divided into 3 deep cut lobes, light green
Flowers	White, 5 petals, one flower per stem, yellow eye
Bloom Time	Spring
Size/Shape	12-18 inches tall, spreading by rhizomes
Special Requirements	Part shade, good drainage, moist soils
Garden Use	Border, edge of woods
Hardiness Zone	4-7
Other Notes	Seed heads looks like cotton balls, may be invasive in some areas
Your Own Notes	_____
	_____
	_____

Anthemis tinctoria

Anthemis tinctoria
(AN-theh-miss tink-TOH-ree-uh)

Common Name	Golden Marguerite; Golden Chamomile
Leaves	Alternate, pinnate, toothed, look like parsley, fragrant when crushed
Flowers	Golden yellow rays and disk flowers
Bloom Time	Summer; June to September
Size/Shape	2-3 feet tall, 2 feet wide
Special Requirements	Full sun, good drainage, short lived in clay soil
Garden Use	Border, cut flowers, best in sandy soils
Hardiness Zone	3-7
Other Notes	'Wargrave' has light yellow flowers (pictured on the left)
Your Own Notes	_____
	_____
	_____

Aquilegia hybrids

Aquilegia hybrids
(ak-wih-LEE-jee-uh)

Common Name	Columbine
Leaves	3-parted leaves with long petiole, gray green color
Flowers	Red, pink, yellow, blue, white, purple; long spurs filled with nectar
Bloom Time	Late spring to early summer
Size/Shape	1-3 feet tall, 12 inch spread
Special Requirements	Full sun to part shade, very good drainage, flowers last longer in part shade. Leaf miner is a problem (pictured upper left).
Garden Use	Borders, leaves ripen in late summer
Hardiness Zone	3-9
Other Notes	*Aquilegia canadensis* has smaller red and yellow flowers (pictured bottom left)
Your Own Notes	_____
	_____
	_____

Arabis caucasica
(AYR-uh-biss kaw-KASS-ih-kuh)

Common Name Rock Cress
Leaves Small, irregular margin, soft hairs, gray green color, evergreen
Flowers White, 4 petals, racemes, fragrant
Bloom Time Early spring
Size/Shape 6-12 inches tall, spreading habit
Special Requirements Full sun, very good drainage (sand and gravel)
Garden Use Rock garden, edging, hanging over retaining walls
Hardiness Zone 4-7
Other Notes 'Snow Caps' is a cultivar with larger flowers
Your Own Notes _____
_____
_____

Armeria maritima

Armeria maritima
(ahr-MEH-ree-uh MAY-ree-tima)

Common Name	Sea Thrift
Leaves	Grass-like leaves, evergreen
Flowers	Pink or white, clusters
Bloom Time	Mid to late spring
Size/Shape	3-4 inches tall, 12 inches tall with the flowers, round mound
Special Requirements	Full sun, very good drainage; avoid clay soils.
Garden Use	Rock gardens, edging, salt tolerant
Hardiness Zone	4-8
Other Notes	
Your Own Notes	_____
	_____
	_____

Artemisia lactiflora

Artemisia lactiflora
(ahr-teh-MIZ-ee-uh; ahr-teh-MEE-zhee-uh lak-tih-FLO-ruh)

Common Name White Mugwort
Leaves Alternate, pinnate, silver gray color, soft to the touch
Flowers Creamy white, not showy
Size/Shape 4-6 feet tall, 3 foot spread, spreads by rhizomes
Special Requirements Full sun, good drainage
Garden Use Background, use for gray foliage
Hardiness Zone 4-8
Other Notes *Artemisia schmidtiana* 'Nana' (Silver Mound) has finely cut, silver foliage (pictured above left)
Your Own Notes _____
_____
_____

Aruncus dioicus

Aruncus dioicus
(uh-RUN-kus dy-EE-kus)

Common Name	Goat's Beard
Leaves	Alternate, pinnate compound, 2-3 feet long, serrate margins
Flowers	White, small, in terminal panicles, looks like Astilbe flowers
Bloom Time	Early summer
Size/Shape	4-6 feet tall, 6 feet wide, looks like a shrub
Special Requirements	Part shade, moist soil
Garden Use	Back of border, wet areas
Hardiness Zone	3-7
Other Notes	
Your Own Notes	_____
	_____
	_____

Asarum europaeum

Asarum europaeum
(ASS-ah-rum yoo-ro-PEE-um)

Common Name	European Ginger
Leaves	Evergreen, round, dark green, shiny, leathery
Flowers	Purple-brown, bell-shaped, hidden by the leaves
Bloom Time	Midspring
Size/Shape	6-10 inches tall, groundcover, spread by rhizomes
Special Requirements	Part shade to shade, moist, acid soils
Garden Use	Perennial border, groundcover in the shade
Hardiness Zone	4-8
Other Notes	*Asarum canadense* (Canadian Ginger) is deciduous with dull green leaves, grows in moist, acidic soils (pictured lower right)
Your Own Notes	_____
	_____
	_____

Asclepias tuberosa

Asclepias tuberosa
(ass-KLEE-pee-us too-bur-O-suh)

Common Name	Butterfly Weed
Leaves	Alternate, long narrow leaves, sessile, hairy
Flowers	Orange, small, in terminal clusters
Bloom Time	Midsummer
Size/Shape	18-36 inches tall, 24 inches wide
Special Requirements	Full sun, dry sandy soils; avoid wet, clay soils
Garden Use	Border, prairie garden, specimen
Hardiness Zone	4-9
Other Notes	Attracts butterflies, difficult to transplant due to taproot
Your Own Notes	_____
	_____
	_____

Aster novae-angliae

Aster novae-angliae
(ASS-tur no-vee-AN-glih-ee; no-veh-AN-glih-ee)

Common Name	New England Aster
Leaves	Alternate, entire, sessile, pubescent
Flowers	Purple, pink, rose or red ray flowers and yellow disk
Bloom Time	Late summer into fall
Size/Shape	4-5 feet tall, 4 feet wide
Special Requirements	Full sun to part shade, good drainage, pinch to keep compact, stake tall cultivars
Garden Use	Border, groups, natural areas, butterfly gardens
Hardiness Zone	4-8
Other Notes	Many cultivars available. 'Purple Dome' is a compact cultivar (pictured above)
Your Own Notes	_____

Astilbe x *arendsii*

Astilbe x *arendsii*
(uh-STIL-bee ahr-END-see-eye)

Common Name	Hybrid Astilbe
Leaves	Compound leaves with double serrate margins
Flowers	Red, pink, white, lavender in panicles
Bloom Time	Early summer
Size/Shape	1-4 feet tall, 2 feet wide
Special Requirements	Part shade is best, moist soil all summer, mulch
Garden Use	Border, edging, groups, divide every 3 years in early spring
Hardiness Zone	4-9
Other Notes	Many cultivars available. A. 'Sprite' has pale pink flowers
Your Own Notes	_____
	_____
	_____

Athyrium georgianum 'Pictum'

Athyrium georgianum 'Pictum'
(a-THEER-ee-um jee-or-jee-AY-num PIK-tum)

Common Name	Japanese Painted Fern
Leaves	Fronds silver gray with reddish stems
Flowers	None
Size/Shape	1-2 feet high, 2 feet wide
Special Requirements	Part shade to full shade, keep moist, mulch
Garden Use	Shade gardens
Hardiness Zone	4-7
Other Notes	
Your Own Notes	_____
	_____
	_____

Baptisia australis

Baptisia australis
(bap-TIZ-ee-uh; bap-TIZH-ee-uh aws-TRAY-liss; aws-TRAW-liss)

Common Name Blue False Indigo

Leaves 3 leaflets, blue-green color

Flowers Blue, pea-like flowers on upright racemes

Bloom Time Midspring

Size/Shape 3-4 feet tall and wide, shrub-like

Special Requirements Full sun to part shade, good drainage

Garden Use Border, background plant

Hardiness Zone 3-9

Other Notes Pod fruit turns black when ripe

Your Own Notes _____

_____

_____

Belamcanda chinensis

Belamcanda chinensis
(bel-am-KAM-duh chin-EN-siss)

Common Name	Blackberry Lily
Leaves	Leaves have parallel veins and look like Bearded Iris, 2 inches wide
Flowers	Orange dotted with red, flowers at the terminals, 6 petals
Bloom Time	Early to midsummer
Size/Shape	2-3 feet tall with flower stalks 4 feet
Special Requirements	Full sun to part shade, good drainage
Garden Use	Perennial border
Hardiness Zone	5-10
Other Notes	Dried capsules open with seeds inside and look like blackberries
Your Own Notes	_____

Bergenia cordifolia

Bergenia cordifolia
(bur-GEN-ee-uh kor-dih-FO-lee-uh)

Common Name	Pigs Squeak
Leaves	Evergreen, large thick fleshy leaves, squeak when rubbed
Flowers	Pink, on stems above the foliage
Bloom Time	Early spring
Size/Shape	12-18 inches tall and clump forming
Special Requirements	Full sun to part shade, good drainage, keep moist
Garden Use	Front of border, possible groundcover
Hardiness Zone	3-8
Other Notes	Winter damage to leaves in northern areas
Your Own Notes	_____
	_____
	_____

Boltonia asteroides
(bohl-TOH-nee-uh ASS-tur-OY-deez)

Common Name	White Boltonia
Leaves	Alternate, narrow, entire, gray-green
Flowers	White rays, yellow disk, small daisy-like flowers forming clouds of white in the fall
Bloom Time	Late summer to fall
Size/Shape	5-6 feet tall, 3-4 feet wide
Special Requirements	Full sun to part shade, good drainage
Garden Use	Perennial border, natural areas
Hardiness Zone	4-9
Other Notes	'Snowbank' is a common cultivar with a compact habit
Your Own Notes	_____

Brunnera macrophylla

Brunnera macrophylla
(brun-NEE-ruh mak-ro-FIL-uh)

Common Name	Bugloss; Heartleaf Brunnera
Leaves	Large heart shaped leaves, rough to the touch
Flowers	Blue, small, similar to *Myosotis* but no yellow eye
Bloom Time	Early spring
Size/Shape	12-18 inches tall, 18 inch spread
Special Requirements	Part shade, good drainage, keep soil moist
Garden Use	Front of border, groups, groundcover
Hardiness Zone	3-8
Other Notes	
Your Own Notes	_____

Calamagrostis x acutiflora

Calamagrostis x acutiflora
(kal-am-uh-**GRAW**-stiss uh-kyoo-tih-**FLOR**-uh)

Common Name Feather Reedgrass
Leaves Dull green grass leaves, rough to the touch
Flowers Light brown, seed heads are stiff and upright, 15 inches long
Bloom Time Early summer
Size/Shape 4-5 feet tall and 2 feet wide
Special Requirements Full sun, good drainage, moist soils, good in clay soils, cut to ground in early spring
Garden Use Groups or mass
Hardiness Zone 4-6
Other Notes 'Karl Foerster' is a popular cultivar that is shorter and earlier to bloom
Your Own Notes _____

_____

_____

Campanula carpatica

Campanula carpatica
(kam-PAN-yoo-luh kahr-PAT-ih-kuh)

Common Name Carpathian Bellflower
Leaves Alternate, simple, triangle shaped, deeply serrate, long petioles
Flowers Blue-lilac, bell-shaped with 5 lobes
Bloom Time Early to midsummer
Size/Shape 9-12 inches tall, spreading clump
Special Requirements Full sun to part shade, good drainage, pinch dead flowers to get more flowers, mulch
Garden Use Front of the perennial border, rock gardens
Hardiness Zone 4-8
Other Notes 'Blue Clips' and 'White Clips' (white flowers) are common cultivars
Your Own Notes _____

_____

Campanula glomerata

Campanula glomerata
(kam-PAN-yoo-luh glom-ur-AYT-uh)

Common Name	Clustered Bellflower
Leaves	Alternate, simple, serrate
Flowers	Purple, bell shaped, clusters at terminals
Bloom Time	Summer
Size/Shape	12-18 inches tall, 12-18 inches wide
Special Requirements	Full sun to part shade, moist soils
Garden Use	Perennial border, groups
Hardiness Zone	3-8
Other Notes	
Your Own Notes	_____

Campanula persicifolia

Campanula persicifolia
(kam-**PAN**-yoo-luh pur-sik-ih-**FO**-lee-uh)

Common Name Peach-leaved Bellflower
Leaves Alternate, simple, lanceolate, 4-8 inches long, serrate, sessile
Flowers Blue, bell-shaped, 5-lobed, solitary on terminal racemes
Bloom Time Late spring to early summer
Size/Shape 2-3 feet tall, 2 feet wide
Special Requirements Full sun to part shade, good drainage, pinch dead flowers to get more flowers, mulch
Garden Use Mass in perennial border
Hardiness Zone 3-7
Other Notes White cultivars are available (pictured lower right)
Your Own Notes _____
_____
_____

Campanula poscharskyana

Campanula poscharskyana
(kam-PAN-yoo-luh po-shar-ski-AY-nuh; pos-char-ski-AY-nuh)

Common Name	Serbian Bellflower
Leaves	Alternate, simple, round, sharply toothed
Flowers	Light blue, star shaped, in panicles
Bloom Time	Late spring to early summer
Size/Shape	8-12 inches tall, 18 inch spread or more
Special Requirements	Full sun to part shade, good drainage
Garden Use	Front of the border, stone walls and rock gardens
Hardiness Zone	3-8
Other Notes	Trailing groundcover
Your Own Notes	

Carex morrowii

Carex morrowii
(KAY-reks mo-ROW-ee-eye)

Common Name	Japanese Sedge
Leaves	Grass-like leaves, triangular stems. Cultivars have green and white stripes or green and gold stripes
Flowers	Not important
Size/Shape	15 inches tall, mound shape
Special Requirements	Part shade to shade, moist soils
Garden Use	Edge of border, groups, rock garden
Hardiness Zone	5-9
Other Notes	'Variegata' is a common cultivar. Pictures are of 'Silk Tassel'
Your Own Notes	_____
	_____
	_____

Catananche caerulea
(kat-uh-NAN-kee seh-ROO-lee-uh)

Common Name	Cupid's Dart
Leaves	Long, narrow grass-like leaves, basal
Flowers	Light purple/blue, single flower, toothed petals, papery texture
Bloom Time	Midsummer
Size/Shape	18-24 inches tall, 12 inches wide
Special Requirements	Full sun, good drainage, avoid clay soils
Garden Use	Mass, rock garden
Hardiness Zone	4-9
Other Notes	Short lived in some areas
Your Own Notes	_____
	_____
	_____

Centaurea dealbata

Centaurea dealbata
(sen-taw-REE-uh; sen-TAW-ree-uh dee-al-BAY-tuh)

Common Name	Persian Cornflower
Leaves	Deeply cut into pinnate lobes, 2 inches long, whitish beneath
Flowers	Pink to lavender, fringe-like
Bloom Time	Early to midsummer
Size/Shape	20-30 inches tall, 18 inches wide, floppy
Special Requirements	Full sun to part shade, good drainage
Garden Use	Perennial border, mass
Hardiness Zone	3-7
Other Notes	May be aggressive in some areas
Your Own Notes	_____
	_____
	_____

Centaurea macrocephala

Centaurea macrocephala
(sen-taw-REE-uh; sen-TAW-ree-uh mak-ro-SEF-a-luh)

Common Name	Globe Centaurea
Leaves	Alternate, large leaves with a wavy margin
Flowers	Yellow, thistle-like, at the terminals, flower buds are scaly brown
Bloom Time	Midsummer
Size/Shape	3-4 feet tall, 2 feet wide
Special Requirements	Full sun, good drainage
Garden Use	Back of the border, specimen
Hardiness Zone	3-8
Other Notes	
Your Own Notes	_____
	_____
	_____

Centaurea montana

Centaurea montana
(sen-taw-REE-uh; sen-TAW-ree-uh mon-TAY-nuh)

Common Name	Perennial Bachelor Button; Mountain Bluet
Leaves	Alternate, simple, wide petiole
Flowers	Blue, single, fringe-like, reddish center
Bloom Time	Early to midsummer
Size/Shape	12-24 inches tall, 12-24 inches wide
Special Requirements	Full sun to part shade, good drainage
Garden Use	Mass in the perennial border
Hardiness Zone	3-8
Other Notes	
Your Own Notes	

Centranthus ruber

Centranthus ruber
(sen-TRAN-thus ROO-bur)

Common Name	Red Valerian
Leaves	Opposite, sessile, blue-green color, waxy
Flowers	Pink-red, small, star-shaped clusters at terminals, fragrant
Bloom Time	Late spring into summer
Size/Shape	18-36 inches tall, 24 inches wide
Special Requirements	Full sun and good drainage, alkaline soils, drought tolerant
Garden Use	Border, natural areas, attracts butterflies
Hardiness Zone	5-8
Other Notes	'Alba' is a white flowering cultivar
Your Own Notes	_____
	_____
	_____

Cephalaria gigantea

Cephalaria gigantea
(sef-uh-LAY-ree-uh jy-gan-TEE-uh; jih-GAN-tee-uh)

Common Name	Tree Scabiosa
Leaves	Opposite, pinnate compound, toothed margin
Flowers	Yellow, on wiry stems above the foliage
Bloom Time	Midsummer
Size/Shape	5-7 feet tall, 3-4 feet wide, loose and open
Special Requirements	Full sun, moist soils
Garden Use	Back of the border
Hardiness Zone	3-8
Other Notes	May self seed and become weedy
Your Own Notes	_____
	_____
	_____

Cerastium tomentosum
(seh-**RAS**-tee-um toh-men-**TOH**-sum)

Common Name Snow-in-Summer

Leaves Opposite, narrow, silver colored, evergreen, small

Flowers White, 5 petals, notched

Bloom Time Midspring

Size/Shape 3-6 inches tall, spreading

Special Requirements Full sun, good drainage, sand and gravel is best

Garden Use Groundcover, rock garden, stone walls

Hardiness Zone 3-7

Other Notes

Your Own Notes _____

_____

_____

Ceratostigma plumbaginoides

Ceratostigma plumbaginoides
(ser-at-o-STIG-muh plum-bah-jih-NOY-deez)

Common Name	Plumbago, Leadwort
Leaves	Alternate, simple, ovate, turn reddish in the fall
Flowers	Blue, 5 petals, small clusters
Bloom Time	Late summer into fall
Size/Shape	8-12 inches tall, 12-18 inch spread
Special Requirements	Full sun to part shade, good drainage
Garden Use	Groundcover, rock garden
Hardiness Zone	5-9
Other Notes	
Your Own Notes	_____
	_____
	_____

Chasmanthium latifolium

Chasmanthium latifolium
(kaz-MAN-thi-um lat-ih-FOE-lee-um)

Common Name	Northern Sea Oats
Leaves	Grass blades 5-9 inches long on stiff stems
Flowers	Bronze seed clusters ripen in late summer and remain through fall
Size/Shape	30-36 inches tall, 12-18 inches wide
Special Requirements	Full sun to part shade, good drainage
Garden Use	Will grow in shade gardens, perennial borders
Hardiness Zone	4-8
Other Notes	Self seeds in sandy soil
Your Own Notes	_____

Chelone lyonii

Chelone lyonii
(kee-LO-nee ly-O-nee-eye)

Common Name	Turtlehead, Shellflower
Leaves	Opposite, simple, serrate, dark green
Flowers	Pink, clusters, looks like turtle's head with its mouth open
Bloom Time	Late summer to early fall
Size/Shape	3 feet tall, 2 feet wide, spreading
	Stiff stems
Special Requirements	Full sun to part shade, moist to wet soil
Garden Use	Near a pond or bog garden, forms dense clumps
Hardiness Zone	3-8
Other Notes	
Your Own Notes	_____
	_____
	_____

Chrysanthemum coccineum

Chrysanthemum coccineum or Pyrethrum roseum or Tanacetum coccineum
(kriss-AN-thee-mum kok-SIN-ee-us — or — py-REE-thrum RO-zee-um —
or — tan-uh-SEE-tum kok-SIN-ee-um)

Common Name	Painted Daisy
Leaves	Deeply cut leaves
Flowers	Red, pink, or white rays, yellow disk flowers, single, on a long stem
Bloom Time	Midsummer
Size/Shape	1-2 feet tall, 1 foot wide
Special Requirements	Full sun to part shade, good drainage, need staking
Garden Use	Natural areas, perennial border, groups
Hardiness Zone	3-7
Other Notes	Short lived in clay soils
Your Own Notes	_____

Chrysanthemum x superbum

Chrysanthemum x superbum, Leucanthemum x superbum
(kriss-AN-thee-mum syoo-PUR-bum — or —
lyoo-KAN-thee-mum syoo-PUR-bum)

Common Name	Shasta Daisy
Leaves	Alternate, oblong, sharp teeth, sessile
Flowers	White rays, yellow disk, long lasting
Bloom Time	Early summer to late summer
Size/Shape	1-3 feet tall, 2 feet wide
Special Requirements	Full sun to part shade, good drainage, divide every 2-3 years
Garden Use	Perennial border in groups
Hardiness Zone	5-9
Other Notes	Deadhead for reblooms
Your Own Notes	_____

Cimicifuga racemosa/Actaea racemosa

Cimicifuga racemosa or *Actaea racemosa*
(sim-ih-SIF-yoo-guh ra-seh-MO-suh; ra-see-MO-suh — or — ak-TEE-uh ra-seh-MO-suh)

Common Name	Snakeroot
Leaves	Large pinnate compound, irregular serrate margins
Flowers	White, small thread-like on 2 foot long racemes, fragrant
Bloom Time	Mid to late summer
Size/Shape	4-6 feet tall, 2-4 feet wide
Special Requirements	Full sun to part shade, moist soil
Garden Use	Back of border, specimen, natural areas
Hardiness Zone	3-8
Other Notes	*C. ramosa* has cultivars with dark maroon leaves (pictured lower left)
Your Own Notes	_____

Clematis hybrids

Clematis hybrids
(KLEM-uh-tiss)

Common Name	Clematis
Leaves	Opposite, pinnate compound, entire, no fall color, stems have ridges
Flowers	White, pink, purple, 4-6 petals
Bloom Time	Late spring to early summer
Size/Shape	5-6 feet high, twining vine, needs support
Special Requirements	Top of the plant needs to be in the sun and the roots in the shade. Mulch, avoid clay soils
Garden Use	Trellis, fences and stone walls
Hardiness Zone	4-8
Other Notes	The best vine for flowers. There are many cultivars with different flower colors
Your Own Notes	_____
	_____
	_____

Convallaria majalis

Convallaria majalis
(kon-va-LAY-ree-uh muh-JAY-liss)

Common Name	Lily of the Valley
Leaves	2 to 3 leaves per stem, parallel veins
Flowers	White, small bell-like on racemes, fragrant
Bloom Time	Midspring
Size/Shape	6-12 inches tall, spreading by rhizomes
Special Requirements	Full to part shade, moist soil is best
Garden Use	Groundcover under trees
Hardiness Zone	2-7
Other Notes	May be aggressive
Your Own Notes	_____

_____

_____

Coreopsis grandiflora

Coreopsis grandiflora
(ko-ree-OP-siss gran-dih-FLOR-uh)

Common Name	Tickseed
Leaves	Opposite, simple, lanceolate, sometimes lobed
Flowers	Yellow, flowers on long stems, yellow rays and yellow or brown disk flowers
Bloom Time	Early to late summer
Size/Shape	2-3 feet tall, 12 inches wide
Special Requirements	Full sun, good drainage, deadhead for rebloom
Garden Use	Perennial border, natural area
Hardiness Zone	4-8
Other Notes	
Your Own Notes	_____
	_____
	_____

Coreopsis verticillata

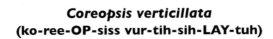

Coreopsis verticillata
(ko-ree-OP-siss vur-tih-sih-LAY-tuh)

Common Name	Threadleaf Coreopsis
Leaves	Thread-like leaves, sessile
Flowers	Yellow, 5 petals, yellow ray and disk flowers
Bloom Time	Late spring to late summer
Size/Shape	2-3 feet tall, 2 feet wide
Special Requirements	Full sun to part shade, dry soils, deadhead for rebloom
Garden Use	Perennial border, natural areas
Hardiness Zone	3-9
Other Notes	'Moonbeam' has creamy yellow flowers
Your Own Notes	_____
	_____
	_____

Corydalis lutea

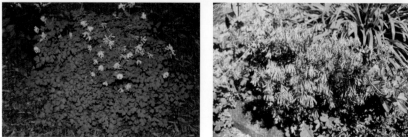

Corydalis lutea
(ko-RID-uh-liss LYOO-tee-uh)

Common Name Yellow Corydalis
Leaves Gray-green, pinnate compound, lobed, fern-like
Flowers Yellow, small tubes in clusters
Bloom Time Late spring to fall
Size/Shape 9-15 inches tall, 18 inches wide. Mound shape
Special Requirements Sun to part shade, good drainage, sand and gravel
Garden Use Rock gardens, stone walls
Hardiness Zone 5-7
Other Notes Self seeds
Corydalis flexuosa has blue flowers (pictured lower right)
Your Own Notes _____
_____
_____

Crambe cordifolia

Crambe cordifolia
(KRAM-bee kor-dih-FO-lee-uh)

Common Name	Colewort
Leaves	Large cabbage-like leaves, hairy and wrinkled
Flowers	White, small, 4 petals, flower in large cluster and looks like Baby's Breath, fragrant
Bloom Time	Late spring to early summer
Size/Shape	6 feet tall, 4 feet wide
Special Requirements	Full sun, good drainage, alkaline soils
Garden Use	Back of border, groups, specimen
Hardiness Zone	5-9
Other Notes	
Your Own Notes	_____

_____

_____

Crambe maritima

Crambe maritima
(KRAM-bee muh-RIT-ih-muh)

Common Name Sea Kale
Leaves Large cabbage-like leaves, gray-green, wavy, evergreen
Flowers White, small, clusters
Bloom Time Early summer
Size/Shape 2 feet tall, 2 feet wide
Special Requirements Full sun, good drainage, salt tolerant
Garden Use Rock garden, specimen
Hardiness Zone 5-9
Other Notes Leaves are edible
Your Own Notes _____
_____
_____

Crocosmia x crocosmiiflora

Crocosmia x crocosmiiflora
(kro-KOZ-mee-uh kro-KOZ-mee-eye-FLOR-uh)

Common Name	Crocosmia/Montbretia
Leaves	Sword-shaped similar to Iris
Flowers	Scarlet (orange-red), one-sided clusters, drooping
Bloom Time	Mid to late summer
Size/Shape	1-3 feet tall, 1 foot wide
Special Requirements	Full sun, good drainage, moist
Garden Use	Perennial border, groups
Hardiness Zone	5-9
Other Notes	Dig corms in the fall and store inside in zone 5
Your Own Notes	_____

Delphinium x *elatum*

Delphinium x *elatum*
(del-FIN-ee-um ee-LAY-tum)

Common Name	Delphinium/Larkspur
Leaves	Large, 5-7 palmate lobes
Flowers	Blue, purple, pink, white, spikes, spur on the back of each flower
Bloom Time	Early to midsummer
Size/Shape	4-6 feet tall, 12-18 inches wide
Special Requirements	Full sun, good drainage, moist, mulch, fertilize often, needs to be staked
Garden Use	Background, specimen
Hardiness Zone	3-7
Other Notes	Many cultivars and hybrids are available
Your Own Notes	_____
	_____
	_____

Dendranthema x morifolium

Dendranthema x morifolium or *Chrysanthemum x morifolium*
(den-DRAN-theh-muh mor-ih-FO-lee-um — or — kriss-AN-thee-mum mor-ih-FO-lee-um)

Common Name	Hardy Mum
Leaves	Lobed with large teeth, strong odor when crushed
Flowers	Wide range of colors, single daisy-like flowers to doubles with many ray flowers
Bloom Time	Late summer to frost
Size/Shape	1-3 feet tall, 1-3 feet wide
Special Requirements	Full sun to part shade, good drainage, fertilize 3 times during season and pinch to keep it compact. Stop pinching after July 4th
Garden Use	Perennial border, mass, seasonal crop in containers
Hardiness Zone	5-9
Other Notes	Also listed as *Chrysanthemum x morifolium* Many cultivars
Your Own Notes	_____ _____

Dianthus barbatus

Dianthus barbatus
(dy-AN-thus bahr-BAY-tus)

Common Name	Sweet William
Leaves	2-3 inch long narrow leaves, short petiole and prominent mid-rib, evergreen
Flowers	Red, pink, white and mixed colors, clusters of fringed flowers with an eye
Bloom Time	Midsummer
Size/Shape	10-18 inches tall, 12 inch spread
Special Requirements	Full sun, good drainage, alkaline soils
Garden Use	Front of perennial border, mass
Hardiness Zone	3-8
Other Notes	Biennial. Many cultivars with different colored flowers
Your Own Notes	_____
	_____
	_____

Dianthus plumarius

Dianthus plumarius
(dy-AN-thus plyoo-MAY-ree-us)

Common Name	Cottage Pinks
Leaves	Gray-green and grass-like, evergreen
Flowers	Rose, pink, white or bi-colored, single or semi-double, fragrant
Bloom Time	Late spring to early summer
Size/Shape	10-12 inches tall, 18-24 inches wide
Special Requirements	Full sun, good drainage, alkaline soils
Garden Use	Rock garden, edging
Hardiness Zone	3-9
Other Notes	Many cultivars available
Your Own Notes	_____
	_____
	_____

Dicentra eximia

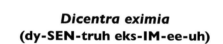

Dicentra eximia
(dy-SEN-truh eks-IM-ee-uh)

Common Name	Fringed Bleeding Heart/Everblooming
Leaves	Pinnate, gray-green, finely cut margins
Flowers	Pink to red, heart shaped, in clusters
Bloom Time	Early summer to fall in moist soils
Size/Shape	12-18 inches tall, 18 inches wide
Special Requirements	Part shade, good drainage, keep moist
Garden Use	Shade border, rock garden, groups
Hardiness Zone	3-9
Other Notes	Many hybrid cultivars available. 'Luxuriant' is a hybrid with cherry-red flowers
Your Own Notes	_____
	_____
	_____

Dicentra spectabilis

Dicentra spectabilis
(dy-SEN-truh spek-TAB-ih-liss)

Common Name Bleeding Heart

Leaves Pinnate compound, leaflets with large teeth on the margins

Flowers Pink, heart shaped with a white arrow coming out of the bottom

Bloom Time Late spring to early summer

Size/Shape 2-3 feet tall, 3 feet wide

Special Requirements Part shade, moist soils, foliage yellows and dies back in hot weather

Garden Use Shade border, plant other plants nearby to hide yellowing foliage

Hardiness Zone 2-9

Other Notes 'Alba' is a white flowering cultivar (pictured lower right)

Your Own Notes _____

_____

_____

Digitalis purpurea

Digitalis purpurea
(dih-jih-TAY-liss pur-PYOO-ree-uh)

Common Name	Foxglove
Leaves	Alternate, large, with a serrate margin, larger at the base, smaller near the top
Flowers	Pink, purple, white, yellow, tube-like, with spots inside, tall raceme
Bloom Time	Late spring to early summer
Size/Shape	2-5 feet tall, 2 feet wide
Special Requirements	Part shade, good drainage, moist, acid soils
Garden Use	Background, natural areas
Hardiness Zone	4-9
Other Notes	Biennial, self seeds, all parts of the plant are poisonous, used for heart medicine
Your Own Notes	_____
	_____

Echinacea purpurea

Echinacea purpurea
(ek-ih-NAY-see-uh pur-PYOO-ree-uh)

Common Name	Purple Coneflower
Leaves	Alternate, arrow shaped, 4-8 inches long, large teeth, rough
Flowers	Purple-pink, pinkish rays drooping, brown disk, one flower per stem
Bloom Time	Summer
Size/Shape	2-4 feet tall, 2 feet wide
Special Requirements	Full sun, good drainage, drought tolerant, deadhead for rebloom
Garden Use	Perennial border, groups, natural areas
Hardiness Zone	3-8
Other Notes	'Magnus' is a common cultivar with petals held out instead of drooping. Plant attracts butterflies
Your Own Notes	_____
	_____
	_____

Echinops ritro

Echinops ritro
(EK-ih-nops RY-troh)

Common Name	Globe Thistle
Leaves	Alternate, lobed margins with a spine at the tips, rough
Flowers	Blue, spiny globe about 2 inches across
Bloom Time	Summer, 6-8 weeks
Size/Shape	3-4 feet tall, 2-3 feet wide
Special Requirements	Full sun, good drainage
Garden Use	Perennial border, specimen
Hardiness Zone	3-8
Other Notes	Can be used as a dried flower
Your Own Notes	_____
	_____
	_____

Epimedium x *versicolor* 'Sulphureum'

Epimedium x *versicolor* 'Sulphureum'
(ep-ih-MEE-dee-um vur-SIK-o-lor sul-FYOO-ree-um)

Common Name	Bicolor Barrenwort
Leaves	Pinnate with 9 leaflets, ovate, entire margin, semi-evergreen, reddish in spring
Flowers	Yellow, small, on racemes, look like miniature daffodils
Bloom Time	Midspring
Size/Shape	8-12 inches tall, spreading by rhizomes
Special Requirements	Part to full shade, good drainage, dry soils
Garden Use	Rock garden, perennial border, dry shade under trees
Hardiness Zone	4-8
Other Notes	
Your Own Notes	

Erigeron hybrids

Erigeron hybrids
(ee-RIH-jur-on)

Common Name	Hybrid Fleabane
Leaves	Alternate, long narrow, winged petiole or sessile
Flowers	Pink to bluish-purple, pink rays and yellow disk
Bloom Time	Midsummer
Size/Shape	18-24 inches tall, 24 inches wide
Special Requirements	Full sun, good drainage is important
Garden Use	Perennial border, rock garden, groups
Hardiness Zone	2-8
Other Notes	Many hybrid cultivars are available. Look like asters
Your Own Notes	_____
	_____
	_____

Eryngium bourgatii

Eryngium bourgatii
(eh-RIN-jee-um boor-GAT-ee-eye)

Common Name	Sea Holly
Leaves	Lobed with a spine at the tips, white veins
Flowers	Blue, surrounded by bracts creating a star-like appearance
Bloom Time	Summer
Size/Shape	18-24 inches tall, 18-24 inches wide
Special Requirements	Full sun, very good drainage, sandy soil is best
Garden Use	Perennial border
Hardiness Zone	5-8
Other Notes	Interesting blue flowers and silver foliage
Your Own Notes	_____

Eupatorium maculatum

Eupatorium maculatum
(yoo-puh-TOH-ree-um mak-yoo-LAY-tum)

Common Name	Spotted Joe Pye Weed
Leaves	Whorled, 3-5 leaves at each node, large, serrate, purple spots on the stem
Flowers	Purple, small, in large clusters at the terminals
Bloom Time	Late summer and fall
Size/Shape	5-7 feet tall, 3-4 feet wide
Special Requirements	Full sun to part shade, moist soils are best
Garden Use	Background, natural areas, near ponds
Hardiness Zone	4-9
Other Notes	*Eupatorium purpureum* is similar but does not have purple spots on the stem
Your Own Notes	_____

Euphorbia cyparissias

Euphorbia cyparissias
(yoo-FOR-bee-uh sih-par-ISS-ee-us)

Common Name	Cypress Spurge
Leaves	Whorled, needle-like leaves, soft, blue-green
Flowers	Yellow changing to reddish, in clusters
Bloom Time	Mid to late spring
Size/Shape	10-12 inches tall, spreading
Special Requirements	Full sun, good drainage, spreads rapidly in rich soil
Garden Use	Rock garden, groundcover, hot dry location
Hardiness Zone	4-8
Other Notes	White sap may irritate the skin
Your Own Notes	_____
	_____
	_____

Euphorbia myrsinites

Euphorbia myrsinites
(yoo-FOR-bee-uh mur-sin-EYE-teez)

Common Name	Myrtle Spurge
Leaves	Whorled, fleshy, blue-green, sessile, evergreen
Flowers	Yellow, showy bracts at terminals
Bloom Time	Spring
Size/Shape	6-8 inches tall, 12-18 inch trailing stems
Special Requirements	Full sun, good drainage, dry rocky soils
Garden Use	Rock garden, stone walls
Hardiness Zone	5-9
Other Notes	
Your Own Notes	_____
	_____
	_____

Euphorbia polychroma

Euphorbia polychroma
(yoo-FOR-bee-uh pah-lee-KRO-muh)

Common Name	Cushion Spurge
Leaves	Alternate, oblong, entire, sessile, turns red in the fall
Flowers	Yellow, showy bracts in clusters at terminals
Bloom Time	Spring
Size/Shape	12-18 inches tall, 18 inches wide
Special Requirements	Full sun, good drainage
Garden Use	Specimen, perennial border, rock gardens
Hardiness Zone	4-8
Other Notes	May be weedy in some areas, toxic sap
Your Own Notes	_____
	_____
	_____

Fallopia japonica var. *compactum*

Fallopia japonica var. *compactum*
(fal-LO-pee-uh juh-PON-ih-kuh kom-PAK-tum)

Common Name	Japanese Knotweed
Leaves	Alternate, oval shape, short petiole, knots on the stem at the nodes
Flowers	Pink, small, in racemes
Bloom Time	Midsummer to frost
Size/Shape	12-18 inches tall, spreading
Special Requirements	Full sun, good drainage
Garden Use	Groundcover
Hardiness Zone	5-9
Other Notes	The cultivar 'Variegatum' (pictured lower right) is common. May be invasive in some areas
Your Own Notes	_____
	_____
	_____

Festuca glauca

Festuca glauca
(fess-TYOO-kuh GLAW-kuh)

Common Name Blue Fescue
Leaves Grass blades, fine, blue color, evergreen
Flowers Light brown seed heads
Size/Shape 6-10 inches tall, 8 inches wide
Special Requirements Full sun, good drainage, avoid clay soils, salt tolerant, cut back to ground in early spring
Garden Use Border, edging, mass
Hardiness Zone 5-8
Other Notes 'Elijah Blue' is a popular cultivar with very blue leaves
Your Own Notes _____
_____
_____

Filipendula rubra

Filipendula rubra
(fil-ih-PEN-dyoo-luh ROO-bruh)

Common Name Queen of the Prairie
Leaves Pinnate compound, leaflets have 5-7 lobes
Flowers Pink to peach, fluffy panicles
Bloom Time Midsummer
Size/Shape 6-8 feet tall, 4 feet wide
Special Requirements Full sun to part shade, good drainage, moist soils
Garden Use Back of the border, specimen, wet areas
Hardiness Zone 3-7
Other Notes *Filipendula ulmaria* is shorter and has white flowers
Your Own Notes _____
_____
_____

Gaillardia x grandiflora

Gaillardia x grandiflora
(gay-LAHR-dee-uh gran-dih-FLOR-uh)

Common Name Blanket Flower

Leaves Alternate, large teeth to lobed margins, coarse stiff hairs, gray-green

Flowers Yellow and red rays and dark red disk flowers

Bloom Time All summer

Size/Shape 2-3 feet tall, 2 foot spread

Special Requirements Full sun, good drainage, short lived in clay soils, deadhead for rebloom

Garden Use Perennial border, groups

Hardiness Zone 3-10

Other Notes 'Goblin' is a compact cultivar

Your Own Notes _____

_____

_____

Gaura lindheimeri

Gaura lindheimeri
(GAW-ruh lind-DYM-mur-eye)

Common Name	Gaura
Leaves	Alternate, narrow, sessile
Flowers	White to pink, 4 petals, on elongating stems
Bloom Time	Early summer to frost
Size/Shape	5 feet tall and wide
Special Requirements	Full sun, good drainage, avoid wet soils
Garden Use	Groups, borders, containers
Hardiness Zone	5-9
Other Notes	Short lived in zone 5
Your Own Notes	_____
	_____
	_____

Geranium x cantabrigiense

Geranium x cantabrigiense
(jeh-RAY-nee-um kan-tuh-brig-ee-ENSS)

Common Name	Cambridge Cranesbill
Leaves	Round shape, deep-cut lobes, irregular teeth
Flowers	White, pink center, 5 petals
Bloom Time	Late spring
Size/Shape	6-8 inches tall, 8 inches wide
Special Requirements	Full sun to part shade, moist soils
Garden Use	Group or mass around small trees, front of the perennial border
Hardiness Zone	5-7
Other Notes	'Biokovo' is a popular cultivar with pinkish white flowers
Your Own Notes	_____

Geranium himalayense

Geranium himalayense
(jeh-RAY-nee-um him-uh-lay-ENSS)

Common Name	Lilac Cranesbill
Leaves	Round shape, deeply divided into 5-7 lobes, 3-6 inches wide
Flowers	Lilac blue, purple veins, 5 petals
Bloom Time	Early summer
Size/Shape	10-15 inches tall, 15 inch spread
Special Requirements	Full sun, good drainage, moist soils
Garden Use	Edge to middle of perennial border
Hardiness Zone	4-8
Other Notes	Geranium x 'Johnson's Blue' is a related hybrid with blue flowers
Your Own Notes	_____
	_____
	_____

Geranium sanguineum

Geranium sanguineum
(jeh-RAY-nee-um san-GWIN-ee-um)

Common Name	Bloody Cranesbill
Leaves	Round with deep cut lobes, 1-2 inches wide
Flowers	Magenta (reddish-purple), 5 petals, single
Bloom Time	Late spring to early summer
Size/Shape	6-12 inches tall, 24 inch spread
Special Requirements	Full sun to part shade, good drainage, moist
Garden Use	Front of border, rock garden
Hardiness Zone	3-8
Other Notes	*Geranium sanguineum* var. *striatum* has pink flowers
Your Own Notes	_____
	_____
	_____

Gypsophila paniculata

Gypsophila paniculata
(jip-SOF-ih-luh pan-ik-yoo-LAY-tuh)

Common Name Baby's Breath

Leaves Opposite, narrow, 4 inches long, gray-green

Flowers White, pale pink, lavender, very small, in large loose and open clusters

Bloom Time Midsummer

Size/Shape 2-3 feet tall, 3 feet wide

Special Requirements Full sun, good drainage, avoid clay soils, does best in high pH soils

Garden Use Perennial border, fill-in when other perennials fade out

Hardiness Zone 3-7

Other Notes Cultivars with double white flowers and pink to lavender flowers are available

Your Own Notes _____

_____

_____

Hakonechloa macra 'Aureola'

Hakonechloa macra 'Aureola'
(ha-kon-ee-KLO-uh MAK-ruh aw-ree-OH-luh)

Common Name Hakone grass
Leaves Grass blades 8-12 inches long, gold with green stripes
Flowers Not important
Size/Shape 12-18 inches tall, weeping mound habit
Special Requirements Full sun to part shade, good drainage, keep moist
Garden Use Mass, group, front of the border, shade gardens
Hardiness Zone 5-9
Other Notes Slow growing, cut back in early spring to promote new growth
Your Own Notes _____
_____
_____

Helenium autumnale

Helenium autumnale
(hel-EE-nee-um aw-tum-NAY-lee)

Common Name	Sneezeweed
Leaves	Alternate, narrow, serrate margin, wings on the stems
Flowers	Yellow, reddish brown, orange, colorful rays, greenish brown disk
Bloom Time	Late summer into fall
Size/Shape	3-5 feet tall, 3 feet wide
Special Requirements	Full sun, good drainage, moist soils
Garden Use	Back of the border
Hardiness Zone	3-8
Other Notes	Many cultivars selected for different flower colors
Your Own Notes	_____
	_____
	_____

Helictotrichon sempervirens

Helictotrichon sempervirens
(hee-lik-toh-TRY-kon sem-pur-VY-renz)

Common Name Blue Oat Grass
Leaves Grass blades 18 inches long, light blue color
Flowers Not important
Size/Shape 2-3 feet tall, 2-3 feet wide
Special Requirements Full sun, good drainage, cut to ground in early spring
Garden Use Perennial border, groups, rock garden
Hardiness Zone 5-8
Other Notes
Your Own Notes _____
_____
_____

Heliopsis helianthoides

Heliopsis helianthoides
(hee-lee-OP-siss hee-lee-an-THOY-deez)

Common Name	Sunflower Heliopsis; Oxeye
Leaves	Opposite, serrate, rough
Flowers	Yellow, rays yellow, disk yellow to brown
Bloom Time	Midsummer
Size/Shape	3-4 feet tall, 4 feet wide
Special Requirements	Full sun to part shade, good drainage, moist soils
Garden Use	Back of the border, natural areas
Hardiness Zone	3-9
Other Notes	Divide every 2-3 years to keep vigorous
Your Own Notes	_____
	_____
	_____

Helleborus niger
(hel-LEB-o-rus NY-jur)

Common Name	Christmas Rose
Leaves	Evergreen, leathery, divided into 7-9 segments, serrate margins
Flowers	White, pink, reddish, cup shaped, drooping
Bloom Time	Early spring to early summer
Size/Shape	15-18 inches tall, 15 inches wide
Special Requirements	Part shade to full shade, good drainage, moist, winter will brown the leaves in zones 3-5
Garden Use	Specimen, perennial shade border
Hardiness Zone	3-9
Other Notes	*Helleborus orientalis* (Lenten Rose) is similar. Many hybrid cultivars are available with different colored flowers
Your Own Notes	_____
	_____
	_____

Hemerocallis hybrids

Hemerocallis hybrids
(hem-ur-o-KAL-iss)

Common Name	Daylily
Leaves	Grass-like, 1-2 feet long and 1 inch wide
Flowers	Many colors, 6 petals, each flower lasts one day
Bloom Time	Early summer to frost
Size/Shape	12 inches to 3-4 feet, depends upon the cultivar
Special Requirements	Full sun to part shade, good drainage
Garden Use	Groups, perennial border, use with shrubs
Hardiness Zone	3-9
Other Notes	Long blooming cultivars such as 'Happy Returns' (picture on top), and 'Stella d' Oro' are popular
Your Own Notes	_____
	_____
	_____

Hesperis matronalis

Hesperis matronalis
(HES-pur-iss ma-tro-NAY-liss)

Common Name	Sweet Rocket
Leaves	Alternate, simple, serrate margin, sessile
Flowers	White, pink, purple, 4 petals, loose raceme, fragrant in the evenings
Bloom Time	Late spring to early summer
Size/Shape	3-4 feet tall, 2 feet wide
Special Requirements	Full sun to part shade, moist soils, high pH soils
Garden Use	Shade gardens, natural areas
Hardiness Zone	3-8
Other Notes	Biennial, self-seeds, may be aggressive in some areas
Your Own Notes	_____
	_____
	_____

Heuchera micrantha

Heuchera micrantha
(HYOO-kur-uh my-KRAN-thuh)

Common Name	Coral Bells
Leaves	Heart shaped, toothed lobes, basal, green to shades of maroon
Flowers	White, pink, red, small bells on long stems above the leaves
Bloom Time	Late spring to early summer
Size/Shape	18 inches tall, 18 inches wide
Special Requirements	Full sun to part shade, good drainage, moist soil, divide every 3 years
Garden Use	Groups, edge of border, use for the colorful foliage
Hardiness Zone	4-9
Other Notes	Many hybrid cultivars with showy leaves. 'Palace Purple' has purple leaves (pictured on the lower left)
Your Own Notes	_____
	_____
	_____

Hibiscus moscheutos
(hy-BISS-kus mos-KEW-tos)

Common Name	Common Rose Mallow
Leaves	Alternate, 8 inches long, ovate, white hairs underneath
Flowers	Red, white, pink, bi-colors, large, 6-12 inches, very showy
Bloom Time	Midsummer
Size/Shape	3-5 feet tall, shrub-like
Special Requirements	Full sun to part shade, moist to wet soils
Garden Use	Specimen, groups, wet areas
Hardiness Zone	4-9
Other Notes	'Kopper King' is a hybrid with red leaves and pink flowers (pictured lower right)
Your Own Notes	_____
	_____
	_____

Hosta hybrids

Hosta hybrids
(HOSS-tuh)

Common Name	Hosta/Plantain Lily
Leaves	Basal leaves, long petiole, heart-shaped to long and narrow, shades of blue, green, yellow and multi-colored
Flowers	White, purple, trumpet shaped, above the foliage, some are fragrant
Bloom Time	Late summer
Size/Shape	Less than 10 inches tall to over 24 inches tall
Special Requirements	Full sun to part shade to shade, moist soils, leaves may scorch in full sun, slugs can be a problem
Garden Use	Perennial border, rock gardens, specimen
Hardiness Zone	3-8
Other Notes	Many cultivars. Pictured are 'Great Expectations' and 'Big Daddy'. 'Patriot' is on the lower left
Your Own Notes	_____

Iberis sempervirens

Iberis sempervirens
(eye-BEE-riss sem-pur-VY-renz)

Common Name	Candytuft
Leaves	Alternate, evergreen, grass-like, stems are woody
Flowers	White, small, 4-petaled, in clusters, covering the plant
Bloom Time	Midspring
Size/Shape	6-12 inches tall, 24 inch spread
Special Requirements	Full sun to part shade, good drainage
Garden Use	Rock garden, edging
Hardiness Zone	3-9
Other Notes	
Your Own Notes	_____

_____
_____

Inula ensifolia

Inula ensifolia
(IN-yoo-luh en-sih-FO-lee-uh)

Common Name Swordleaf Inula
Leaves Alternate, narrow, 4 inches long, sessile
Flowers Yellow, single, yellow rays and yellow disk
Bloom Time Early summer for 6 weeks
Size/Shape 12-24 inches tall, 18 inches wide
Special Requirements Full sun to part shade, good drainage
Garden Use Front of border
Hardiness Zone 3-8
Other Notes Nice neat habit
Your Own Notes _____

_____

_____

Iris hybrids
(EYE-riss)

Common Name	Bearded Iris
Leaves	Sword-shaped, 1½ feet long and 1½ inches wide, gray-green
Flowers	Many colors, 3 standards (upright petals) and 3 falls (drooping petals), beard on the falls
Bloom Time	Late spring to early summer
Size/Shape	2-4 feet tall, clump forming
Special Requirements	Full sun to part shade, good drainage, avoid clay soils, iris borer is a problem
Garden Use	Perennial or mixed border
Hardiness Zone	3-10
Other Notes	Root rot is a problem, divide every 3 years
Your Own Notes	

Iris sibirica

Iris sibirica
(EYE-riss sy-BIR-ih-kuh)

Common Name	Siberian Iris
Leaves	Narrow grass-like leaves, yellow fall color
Flowers	White, blue, purple, violet, 3 standards (upright petals) and 3 falls (drooping petals)
Bloom Time	Late spring
Size/Shape	24-36 inches tall, 24 inches wide
Special Requirements	Full sun to part shade, good drainage to moist soils
Garden Use	Perennial border, groups
Hardiness Zone	3-9
Other Notes	Resistant to iris borer and root rot
Your Own Notes	_____

Knautia macedonica

Knautia macedonica
(NAW-tee-uh mass-sih-DON-ih-kuh)

Common Name Knautia
Leaves Entire margins at base of plant, lobed near the top
Flowers Pink, red or reddish-purple, pincushion-like on long stems
Bloom Time Early summer to fall
Size/Shape 2-3 feet tall, 2 feet wide, loose and open
Special Requirements Full sun, good drainage, deadhead for rebloom
Garden Use Middle of the border, natural areas
Hardiness Zone 4-7
Other Notes Short lived
Your Own Notes _____
_____
_____

Kniphofia hybrids

Kniphofia hybrids
(nip-HO-fee-uh; ny-FO-fee-uh)

Common Name	Torch Lily, Red Hot Poker
Leaves	Sword-like, 3 feet long, gray-green
Flowers	Red, orange, yellow, tubular small flowers in racemes at the end of the stem
Bloom Time	Midsummer
Size/Shape	2-4 feet tall, 3 feet wide
Special Requirements	Full sun, good drainage, avoid clay soils
Garden Use	Specimen, groups
Hardiness Zone	5-9
Other Notes	
Your Own Notes	_____
	_____
	_____

Lamium maculatum

Lamium maculatum
(LAY-mee-um mak-yoo-LAY-tum)

Common Name	Dead Nettle
Leaves	Opposite, triangular, green margin with silver center, square stem
Flowers	Mauve, pink, small tube with a hood, in clusters
Bloom Time	Late spring to midsummer
Size/Shape	8-12 inches tall, trailing
Special Requirements	Part to full shade, good drainage, moist soils
Garden Use	Groundcover for shade, edging
Hardiness Zone	3-8
Other Notes	Planted for showy foliage, some cultivars have white flowers
Your Own Notes	_____
	_____
	_____

Lavandula angustifolia

Lavandula angustifolia
(luh-VAN-dyoo-luh an-gus-tih-FO-lee-uh)

Common Name	Lavender
Leaves	Opposite or whorled, 2 inches long, narrow, gray-green, evergreen, square stems, fragrant when crushed
Flowers	Lavender or purple, small flowers in spikes, fragrant
Bloom Time	Early summer
Size/Shape	12-24 inches tall, round shape
Special Requirements	Full sun, good drainage, avoid clay soils, deadhead for rebloom
Garden Use	Rock garden, groups, small hedge
Hardiness Zone	5-9
Other Notes	Some cultivars have white flowers
Your Own Notes	_____
	_____
	_____

Liatris spicata

Liatris spicata
(ly-AY-triss spy-KAY-tuh)

Common Name Gayfeather, Blazing Star
Leaves Alternate, basal leaves 10-12 inches long, narrow grass-like
Flowers Rose, lavender, white, 6-15 inch long flower spike with small individual flowers, flowers open from the top down
Bloom Time Midsummer
Size/Shape 1-3 feet tall, 24 inches wide
Special Requirements Sun to part shade, good drainage, avoid clay soils
Garden Use Perennial border, groups
Hardiness Zone 3-9
Other Notes 'Kobold' is a compact cultivar
Your Own Notes _____
_____
_____

Ligularia stenocephala

Ligularia stenocephala
(lig-yoo-LAY-ree-uh sten-o-SEF-uh-luh)

Common Name	Ligularia
Leaves	Basal, round to triangular, large, 8-12 inches long, toothed, petioles purple-black
Flowers	Yellow, rays yellow, disk yellow, tall racemes
Bloom Time	Midsummer
Size/Shape	5-6 feet tall, flowers above the leaves
Special Requirements	Full sun to part shade, moist to wet soils
Garden Use	Specimen, near ponds
Hardiness Zone	5-8
Other Notes	'The Rocket' is more compact with lemon yellow flowers
Your Own Notes	_____
	_____
	_____

Lilium hybrids

Lilium hybrids
(LIL-ee-um)

Common Name Lily
Leaves Narrow leaves along the stem, parallel veins
Flowers Many colors: white, orange, red, pink, yellow; 6 petals
Bloom Time Early to midsummer
Size/Shape 2-6 feet tall, single stems
Special Requirements Full sun to part shade, good drainage, mulch, plant bulbs in the fall 8 inches deep, bulbs rot in wet soils
Garden Use Groups, mass
Hardiness Zone 5-9
Other Notes Bulbs are planted in the fall for spring flowers, many are fragrant
Your Own Notes _____
_____
_____

Linaria purpurea

Linaria purpurea
(ly-NAY-ree-uh pur-PYOO-ree-uh)

Common Name	Toad Flax
Leaves	Whorled, narrow, blue-green
Flowers	Blue-purple, snapdragon-like, single spur at the base of each flower, in spikes
Bloom Time	All summer
Size/Shape	2-3 feet tall, vertical narrow shape
Special Requirements	Full sun to part shade, good drainage, avoid clay soils
Garden Use	Borders, groups
Hardiness Zone	5-9
Other Notes	Not hardy in zone 5 but will come back from seed each year
Your Own Notes	_____
	_____
	_____

Linum flavum

Linum flavum
(LY-num FLAY-vum)

Common Name	Golden Flax
Leaves	Narrow, lanceolate, leathery
Flowers	Yellow, 1 inch wide, waxy, in clusters
Bloom Time	Early summer
Size/Shape	15-18 inches tall, 12 inches wide
Special Requirements	Full sun, good drainage
Garden Use	Front of perennial border, rock garden
Hardiness Zone	5-7
Other Notes	
Your Own Notes	_____

_____

_____

Linum perenne

Linum perenne
(LY-num pur-EN-nee)

Common Name	Perennial Flax
Leaves	Alternate, lanceolate, 1 inch long, blue-gray
Flowers	Sky blue, 5 petals, each flower lasts one day
Bloom Time	Late spring to summer
Size/Shape	24 inches tall, 12-18 inches wide, arching habit
Special Requirements	Full sun, good drainage, avoid clay soils
Garden Use	Rock garden, perennial border
Hardiness Zone	5-8
Other Notes	May not live very long
Your Own Notes	_____
	_____
	_____

Liriope spicata
(lih-RY-o-pee spy-KAY-tuh)

Common Name Creeping Lily-Turf

Leaves Evergreen, narrow grass-like leaves

Flowers Lilac-purple, dense spikes above the leaves, glossy

Bloom Time Late summer

Size/Shape 12-18 inches high, 12 inches wide, spreads by stolons

Special Requirements Full sun to full shade, good drainage, mow in early spring to remove old leaves

Garden Use Groundcover for shade

Hardiness Zone 4-9

Other Notes *Liriope muscari* (Blue Lily-Turf) is similar with wider leaves and hardy to zone 6-9

Your Own Notes _____
_____
_____

Lobelia cardinalis

Lobelia cardinalis
(lo-BEE-lee-uh; lo-BEEL-yuh kahr-dih-NAY-liss)

Common Name	Cardinal Flower
Leaves	Alternate, lanceolate, serrate margin, sessile
Flowers	Scarlet, tube with reflexed petals, racemes
Bloom Time	Midsummer
Size/Shape	3-4 feet tall, 2 feet wide
Special Requirements	Part shade, moist soils, mulch, attracts butterflies and hummingbirds
Garden Use	Perennial border, natural areas
Hardiness Zone	3-9
Other Notes	Short lived
Your Own Notes	_____
	_____
	_____

Lupinus hybrids
(lyoo-PY-nus)

Common Name	Lupine
Leaves	Palmate compound, 9-16 leaflets, long petiole
Flowers	Many colors, flowers in terminal racemes
Bloom Time	Early summer
Size/Shape	3-4 feet tall, 12-14 inches wide
Special Requirements	Full sun to part shade, moist soils, best in cool areas, acid soils
Garden Use	Perennial border, needs staking
Hardiness Zone	4-6
Other Notes	'Russell Hybrid' is a common cultivar with many different colored flowers (pictured)
Your Own Notes	_____

Lychnis chalcedonica

Lychnis chalcedonica
(LIK-niss chal-see-DON-ih-kuh)

Common Name	Maltese Cross
Leaves	Opposite, simple, lanceolate, leaves clasping the stem, rough hairy leaves
Flowers	Scarlet, terminal clusters 3-4 inches wide
Bloom Time	Summer
Size/Shape	2-3 feet tall, 18 inch spread
Special Requirements	Full sun to part shade, good drainage, moist, short lived
Garden Use	Groups, perennial border
Hardiness Zone	3-9
Other Notes	Short-lived in clay soils. *Lychnis x arkwrightii* has similar orange-red flowers with maroon leaves
Your Own Notes	_____
	_____
	_____

Lychnis coronaria

Lychnis coronaria
(LIK-niss kor-o-NAY-ree-uh)

Common Name Rose Campion
Leaves Opposite, oblong, gray-green, pubescent
Flowers Magenta, single flowers, 5 petals, on long stems
Bloom Time Late spring to early summer
Size/Shape 2-3 tall, 18 inches wide
Special Requirements Full sun, good drainage, short-lived, self seeds
Garden Use Perennial border
Hardiness Zone 4-8
Other Notes
Your Own Notes _____
_____
_____

Lychnis viscaria

Lychnis viscaria
(LIK-niss viss-KAY-ree-uh)

Common Name	Catchfly
Leaves	Grass-like, basal
Flowers	Magenta to pink, clusters, flower stem is sticky
Bloom Time	Late spring
Size/Shape	12-15 inches tall, 8-10 inches wide
Special Requirements	Full sun to part shade, good drainage
Garden Use	Front of border, groups, rock gardens
Hardiness Zone	3-7
Other Notes	'Alba' has white flowers (pictured on the bottom)
Your Own Notes	_____
	_____
	_____

Lysimachia clethroides

Lysimachia clethroides
(ly-sih-MAY-kee-uh; liss-ih-MAK-ee-uh kleth-ROY-deez)

Common Name Gooseneck Loosestrife

Leaves Alternate, simple, ovate-lanceolate, stems and leaves pubescent

Flowers White, star-shaped on curved raceme, looks like a goose neck

Bloom Time Early summer

Size/Shape 2-3 feet tall, spreads by rhizomes

Special Requirements Full sun to part shade, good drainage, moist

Garden Use Aggressive near ponds, needs to be restricted

Hardiness Zone 3-8

Other Notes

Your Own Notes _____

_____

_____

Lysimachia nummularia

Lysimachia nummularia
(ly-sih-MAY-kee-uh; liss-ih-MAK-ee-uh num-yoo-LAY-ree-uh)

Common Name	Moneywort; Creeping Jenny
Leaves	Opposite, round, 1 inch long, 'Aurea' (pictured) has gold leaves
Flowers	Yellow, cup shaped
Bloom Time	Late spring
Size/Shape	2-4 inches tall, spreads 24 inches
Special Requirements	Full sun to shade, moist soils
Garden Use	Groundcover for wet areas, stone walls, containers
Hardiness Zone	3-8
Other Notes	
Your Own Notes	

Lysimachia punctata

Lysimachia punctata
(ly-sih-MAY-kee-uh; liss-ih-MAK-ee-uh punk-TAY-tuh)

Common Name	Yellow Loosestrife
Leaves	Whorled, ovate-lanceolate, entire margin, pubescent
Flowers	Yellow, cup shaped, 5 petals, clustered in leaf axils
Bloom Time	Late spring to early summer
Size/Shape	18-30 inches tall, 12 inches wide
Special Requirements	Full sun to part shade, moist soils
Garden Use	Perennial border, needs room to spread
Hardiness Zone	4-8
Other Notes	May be invasive in some areas
Your Own Notes	_____
	_____
	_____

Lythrum salicaria

Lythrum salicaria
(LITH-rum sal-ih-KAY-ree-uh)

Common Name Purple Loosestrife
Leaves Opposite or whorled, lanceolate, clasping the stem
Flowers Purplish-pink, spikes 1 foot long
Bloom Time Mid to late summer
Size/Shape 3-5 feet tall, 2-3 feet wide
Special Requirements Full sun, wet or dry soils, deadhead to prevent seeding
Garden Use Invasive in wet areas
Hardiness Zone 3-9
Other Notes Should not plant
Your Own Notes _____

Macleaya cordata

Macleaya cordata
(mak-LAY-uh kor-DAY-tuh)

Common Name	Plume Poppy
Leaves	Alternate, simple, lobed, gray-green on top, gray-brown on lower surface
Flowers	Cream, small, in terminal clusters
Bloom Time	Mid to late summer
Size/Shape	6-10 feet tall, 6 feet wide, shrub-like
Special Requirements	Full sun to part shade, good drainage, moist, no staking needed
Garden Use	Back of border, specimen
Hardiness Zone	3-8
Other Notes	
Your Own Notes	_____

Malva alcea

Malva alcea
(MAL-vuh al-SEE-uh; AL-see-uh)

Common Name	Hollyhock Mallow
Leaves	Alternate, 3-5 lobes, deeply cut, pubescent
Flowers	Pink, 5 petals, each one has a notch, in spikes
Bloom Time	Early summer for 6-8 weeks
Size/Shape	3-4 feet tall, 18 inches wide
Special Requirements	Full sun to part shade, good drainage, short lived, self seeds
Garden Use	Perennial border
Hardiness Zone	4-8
Other Notes	'Fastigiata' is more upright
Your Own Notes	

Mertensia virginica

Mertensia virginica
(mur-TEN-see-uh vur-JIN-ih-kuh)

Common Name	Virginia Bluebells
Leaves	Alternate, basal leaves, entire margin, ripen in late spring
Flowers	Blue-purple, trumpet-shaped, in clusters
Bloom Time	Early spring
Size/Shape	12-24 inches tall, clump forming
Special Requirements	Shade, good drainage, moist
Garden Use	Shade gardens, rock gardens, perennial border
Hardiness Zone	3-9
Other Notes	Foliage dies down in late spring; should be planted with other plants to fill the space
Your Own Notes	_____

Miscanthus sinensis

Miscanthus sinensis
(miss-KAN-thus sy-NEN-siss)

Common Name Japanese Silver Grass
Leaves Grass blades 3-4 feet long, basal, serrate, white midvein, reddish fall color
Flowers Light pink to silver, terminal panicles, persist into winter
Bloom Time Late fall
Size/Shape 4-8 feet tall, 3-4 foot spread, clump
Special Requirements Full sun, good drainage, comes up late in the spring
Garden Use Specimen, screen, mass
Hardiness Zone 5-9
Other Notes 'Zebrinus' (pictured on the left)
Your Own Notes _____

_____

_____

Monarda didyma

Monarda didyma
(mo-NAR-duh DID-ih-muh)

Common Name Bee Balm

Leaves Opposite, ovate, serrate, fragrant when crushed, square stems

Flowers Red, pink, purple, white, tubular flowers in clusters forming a head

Bloom Time Midummer

Size/Shape 2-4 feet tall, 3 feet wide, spreading by rhizomes

Special Requirements Full sun to part shade, good drainage, moist, mildew is a problem

Garden Use Perennial border, natural areas (divide every 3 years to contain)

Hardiness Zone 4-9

Other Notes 'Petite Delight' (pictured on left), 'Marshall's Delight' (pictured on right) both mildew resistant

Your Own Notes _____

_____

_____

Myosotis sylvatica

Myosotis sylvatica
(my-o-SO-tiss sil-VAT-ih-kuh)

Common Name Forget-Me-Not
Leaves Alternate, simple, entire, oblong-linear, sessile, small, hairy
Flowers Blue, yellow center, small, in clusters
Bloom Time Spring
Size/Shape 6-8 inches tall, 6 inches wide
Special Requirements Part shade is best, good drainage, moist, self-seeds
Garden Use Plant around bulbs, perennial border, natural areas
Hardiness Zone 3-8
Other Notes
Your Own Notes _____
_____
_____

Nepeta x faassenii

Nepeta x faassenii
(NEP-eh-tuh ex fah-SEEN-ee-eye; NEP-eh-tuh fah-SEEN-ee-eye)

Common Name Catmint, Nepeta

Leaves Opposite, oblong, serrate, silvery green, pubescent, fragrant when crushed, square stems

Flowers Lavender to blue, trumpet shaped, 2-lipped, in racemes

Bloom Time Late spring to early summer, prune after bloom for re-bloom late summer

Size/Shape 18-36 inches tall, spreading, depends upon cultivar

Special Requirements Full sun to part shade, good drainage

Garden Use Front of border, groups

Hardiness Zone 3-8

Other Notes 'Six Hills Giant' is a common cultivar with upright stems and larger size

Your Own Notes _____

_____

_____

Oenothera macrocarpa (missouriensis)

Oenothera macrocarpa (missouriensis)
(ee-no-THEE-ruh; ee-NOTH-ur-uh mak-ro-KAHR-puh [miss-ZUR-ee-EN-sis])

Common Name	Missouri Evening Primrose
Leaves	Alternate, long narrow blades, entire margin
Flowers	Bright yellow, 3-4 inches wide, slight fragrance
Bloom Time	Early summer
Size/Shape	9-12 inches tall, 12 inches wide, trailing
Special Requirements	Full sun, good drainage, avoid clay soils
Garden Use	Raised bed, rock garden, edge of walks
Hardiness Zone	3-7
Other Notes	Colorful seed pods
Your Own Notes	_____

Oenothera speciosa

Oenothera speciosa
(ee-no-THEE-ruh; ee-NOTH-ur-uh spee-see-O-suh)

Common Name	Showy Evening Primrose
Leaves	Alternate, narrow, 3 inches long, pubescent
Flowers	Pink, white, 4 petals, cup shaped
Bloom Time	Summer
Size/Shape	6-24 inches tall, spreading
Special Requirements	Full sun to part shade, very good drainage, weedy in fertile soils
Garden Use	Edge of road or sidewalk, aggressive in perennial border
Hardiness Zone	3-8
Other Notes	
Your Own Notes	_____
	_____
	_____

Oenothera tetragona (fruticosa ssp. glauca)

Oenothera tetragona (fruticosa ssp. glauca)
(ee-no-THEE-ruh; ee-NOTH-ur-uh tet-ruh-GO-nuh)
[(froo-tih-KO-suh subspecies GLAW-kuh]

Common Name	Common Sundrops
Leaves	Long narrow leaves, entire margin, hairy, sessile
Flowers	Yellow, cup shaped, terminal clusters
Bloom Time	Early summer
Size/Shape	18-24 inches tall, 24 inches wide
Special Requirements	Full sun, good drainage
Garden Use	Edge of border, group
Hardiness Zone	4-8
Other Notes	May spread quickly
Your Own Notes	_____

_____
_____

Opuntia humifusa

Opuntia humifusa
(o-PUN-tee-uh hyoo-mih-FYOO-suh)

Common Name	Prickly Pear Cactus
Leaves	Thick fleshy stems, sharp spines, evergreen
Flowers	Yellow, at the end of the stems, each flower lasts one day
Bloom Time	Early summer
Size/Shape	8-12 inches tall, clump forming
Special Requirements	Full sun, very good drainage, avoid clay soils
Garden Use	Rock garden, stone wall
Hardiness Zone	5-10
Other Notes	
Your Own Notes	_____

Paeonia hybrids

Paeonia hybrids
(pee-O-nee-uh)

Common Name	Hybrid Peony
Leaves	Alternate, pinnate, leaflets entire or lobed
Flowers	Many colors (depends upon cultivar), 3-6 inches across, fragrant, single, semi-double, and double
Bloom Time	Late spring to early summer
Size/Shape	3 feet tall, 3 feet wide, shrub-like
Special Requirements	Full sun to part shade, good drainage, mulch
Garden Use	Specimen, perennial border
Hardiness Zone	3-8
Other Notes	Many cultivars available with a wide range of colors
Your Own Notes	_____
	_____
	_____

Paeonia suffruticosa

Paeonia suffruticosa
(pee-O-nee-uh suh-froo-tih-KO-suh)

Common Name	Tree Peony
Leaves	Alternate, pinnate, leaflets 3-5 lobes, whitish beneath
Flowers	Red, rose pink, white, yellow, 6-8 inches across
Bloom Time	Midspring, don't last long
Size/Shape	3-5 feet tall, 3-4 feet wide, woody stems, shrub
Special Requirements	Full sun to part shade, good drainage, mulch
	More shade tolerant than herbaceous peonies
Garden Use	Specimen
Hardiness Zone	4-7
Other Notes	Many cultivars available. Does not die to the ground in winter
Your Own Notes	_____
	_____
	_____

Panicum virgatum

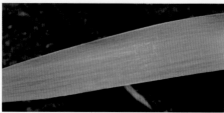

Panicum virgatum
(PAN-ih-kum vur-GAY-tum)

Common Name	Switch Grass
Leaves	Grass blades 2-3 feet long
Flowers	Large panicles, loose and open
Bloom Time	Mid to late summer
Size/Shape	4-5 feet tall, clump forming, columnar
Special Requirements	Full sun, wet or dry soils, salt tolerant, cut back to ground in early spring
Garden Use	Groups, mass, screen, natural areas
Hardiness Zone	5-9
Other Notes	'Heavy Metal' has blue-green leaves
Your Own Notes	_____
	_____
	_____
	_____

Papaver orientale

Papaver orientale
(puh-PAY-vur or-ee-en-TAY-lee)

Common Name	Oriental Poppy
Leaves	Deeply cut fern-like leaves, hairy, dieback in midsummer
Flowers	Red, orange, pink, white, 4-6 papery petals, black stamens in the center
Bloom Time	Late spring
Size/Shape	2-4 feet tall, 2-4 feet wide
Special Requirements	Full sun to part shade, good drainage, plant other plants nearby to hide dying foliage
Garden Use	Perennial border
Hardiness Zone	3-7
Other Notes	
Your Own Notes	

Pennisetum alopecuroides

Pennisetum alopecuroides
(pen-ih-SEE-tum a-lo-peh-kyur-OY-deez)

Common Name Fountain Grass

Leaves Grass blades 20-24 inches long, turn yellow in the fall

Flowers Foxtail-like flowers, copper bronze to dark purple

Bloom Time Late summer into fall

Size/Shape 24-30 inches tall, 24 inches wide

Special Requirements Full sun, good drainage, cut back to ground in early spring

Garden Use Group, mass

Hardiness Zone 5-9

Other Notes 'Hameln' is a compact cultivar. The annual *P. setaceum* has purple leaf cultivars that are popular

Your Own Notes _____

_____

_____

Penstemon digitalis

Penstemon digitalis
(pen-STEE-mon; PEN-stee-mon dih-jih-TAY-liss)

Common Name	Beardtongue
Leaves	4-5 inches long, oblong-lanceolate, often reddish in the spring
Flowers	White, pink, tubular with 2 lips, in terminal racemes
Bloom Time	Late spring to midsummer
Size/Shape	2-3 feet tall, 18 inches wide
Special Requirements	Full sun to part shade, good drainage
Garden Use	Perennial border, mass, natural areas
Hardiness Zone	3-8
Other Notes	'Husker Red' (pictured) has white flowers and reddish leaves
Your Own Notes	_____
	_____
	_____

Perovskia atriplicifolia

Perovskia atriplicifolia
(peh-ROF-skee-uh at-rih-plih-sih-FOL-lee-uh)

Common Name	Russian Sage
Leaves	Opposite, deeply cut leaves, gray-white beneath, fragrant when crushed, silver stems
Flowers	Lavender-blue, tubular, 2-lipped, in panicles
Bloom Time	Mid to late summer for 10 weeks
Size/Shape	3-4 feet tall, 3-4 feet wide
Special Requirements	Full sun, good drainage, avoid clay soils, cut back to ground in early spring
Garden Use	Group, mass, filler in perennial border
Hardiness Zone	5-9
Other Notes	
Your Own Notes	_____

Phalaris arundinacea

Phalaris arundinacea
(FAL-uh-riss uh-run-dih-NAY-see-uh)

Common Name Ribbon Grass
Leaves Grass blades 6-12 inches long
Flowers Not important
Size/Shape 24-36 inches tall, spreading by rhizomes
Special Requirements Full sun to part shade, wet or dry soils, leaves brown
in late summer
Garden Use Invasive, plant in restricted areas
Hardiness Zone 4-9
Other Notes 'Picta' has variegated leaves (pictured) and is the most
common cultivar
Your Own Notes _____
_____
_____

Phlox maculata

Phlox maculata
(FLOKS mak-yoo-LAY-tuh)

Common Name	Meadow Phlox
Leaves	Opposite, 2-4 inches long, narrow to oblong, thick, glossy dark green, spotted stems
Flowers	Pinkish-purple, 5 petals, in conical clusters, fragrant
Bloom Time	Early summer
Size/Shape	24-36 inches tall, 24 inches wide
Special Requirements	Full sun to part shade, good drainage, mulch, mildew resistant
Garden Use	Perennial border, attracts butterflies and hummingbirds
Hardiness Zone	3-8
Other Notes	*Phlox paniculata* is more common, with many cultivars. It differs by having blooms in late summer and is prone to powdery mildew
Your Own Notes	_____
	_____
	_____

Phlox paniculata

Phlox paniculata
(FLOKS pan-ik-yoo-LAY-tuh)

Common Name Garden Phlox

Leaves Opposite, 2-5 inches long, long pointed tip

Flowers Many different colors, often pink to lavender, tubular with 5 petals in dense cone shaped clusters, fragrant

Bloom Time Midsummer

Size/Shape 3-4 feet high, 2 feet wide

Special Requirements Full sun to part shade, good drainage, good air circulation, moist soils
Powdery mildew can be a problem

Garden Use Perennial border, attracts butterflies and hummingbirds

Hardiness Zone 4-8

Other Notes Many cultivars available with a wide range of flower colors. Select mildew resistant plants

Your Own Notes _____

_____

Phlox subulata

Phlox subulata
(FLOKS sub-yoo-LAY-tuh)

Common Name Moss Phlox
Leaves Opposite, needle-like leaves, ½ inch long, evergreen
Flowers Pink, blue, white, purple, 5 notched petals, terminal clusters, fragrant
Bloom Time Midspring
Size/Shape 3-6 inches tall, trailing
Special Requirements Full sun to part shade, good drainage, avoid clay soils
Garden Use Edge of beds, raised beds, rock walls
Hardiness Zone 3-9
Other Notes Many cultivars
Your Own Notes _____
_____
_____

Physostegia virginiana

Physostegia virginiana
(fy-so-STEE-jee-uh vur-jin-ee-AY-nuh)

Common Name	Obedient Plant
Leaves	Opposite, oblong to lanceolate, serrate, square stem
Flowers	Rose-purple, white, tubular, in terminal spikes, arranged in 4 rows
Bloom Time	Late summer into fall
Size/Shape	2-4 feet tall, 3 feet wide or more
Special Requirements	Full sun to part shade, moist soils, may be invasive
Garden Use	Natural areas, wildflower gardens
Hardiness Zone	3-9
Other Notes	May be aggressive, restrict growth
Your Own Notes	_____

Platycodon grandiflorus

Platycodon grandiflorus
(plat-ih-KO-don gran-dih-FLOR-us)

Common Name	Balloonflower
Leaves	Alternate to whorled, ovate, serrate, 1-3 inches long, blue green
Flowers	Blue, white, pink, flower buds are balloon-shaped, open to saucer-shape with 5 pointed lobes
Bloom Time	Midsummer
Size/Shape	24-36 inches tall, 24 inches wide
Special Requirements	Full sun to part shade, good drainage, avoid wet clay soils, emerges late in the spring
Garden Use	Perennial border, rock gardens
Hardiness Zone	3-8
Other Notes	Slow growing but long lived
Your Own Notes	_____

Polemonium caeruleum

Polemonium caeruleum
(po-leh-MO-nee-um seh-ROO-lee-um; see-ROO-lee-um)

Common Name Jacob's Ladder
Leaves Alternate, basal, odd-pinnate, leaflets sessile
Flowers Blue, pink, white, cup shaped, in clusters
Bloom Time Late spring
Size/Shape 18-24 inches tall, 18 inches wide
Special Requirements Full sun to part shade, good drainage, best in cool shade, keep moist
Garden Use Rock garden, perennial border, groups, shade garden
Hardiness Zone 3-7
Other Notes
Your Own Notes _____
_____
_____

Polygonatum biflorum

Polygonatum biflorum
(po-lig-o-NAY-tum by-FLOR-um)

Common Name	Small Solomon's Seal
Leaves	Alternate, sessile, ovate, parallel veins
Flowers	Greenish white, in pairs, hang down like small bells
Bloom Time	Late spring
Size/Shape	2-3 feet tall, arching stems, spreads by rhizomes
Special Requirements	Shade, good drainage, moist
Garden Use	Shade gardens
Hardiness Zone	3-9
Other Notes	*Polygonatum odoratum* 'Variegatum' has green and white leaves (pictured on lower left)
Your Own Notes	

Polygonum affine (Persicaria affinis)

Polygonum affine (Persicaria affinis)
(po-LIG-o-num a-FY-nee) [pur-sih-KAY-ree-uh a-FY-niss]

Common Name Fleeceflower
Leaves Basal leaves, long narrow, with a white midvein, fine serrations
Flowers Rose-pink, small, in a spike 2-3 inches long
Bloom Time Midsummer
Size/Shape 6-9 inches tall, 12 inches wide, groundcover
Special Requirements Full sun to part shade, moist soils
Garden Use Front of border, rock garden, pond edge
Hardiness Zone 3-7
Other Notes 'Darjeeling Red' is a common cultivar with dark pink flowers
Your Own Notes _____
_____
_____

Pulmonaria saccharata

Pulmonaria saccharata
(puhl-mo-NAY-ree-uh sak-uh-RAY-tuh)

Common Name	Bethlehem Sage
Leaves	Alternate, basal, ovate, hairy, white spots
Flowers	Pink change to blue, funnel-shaped, in clusters
Bloom Time	Early to midspring
Size/Shape	12-18 inches tall, 24 inches wide
Special Requirements	Full to part shade, cool moist soils, mulch
Garden Use	Specimen or groups in shade garden
Hardiness Zone	3-8
Other Notes	Many cultivars selected for the showy leaves
Your Own Notes	_____

Ranunculus repens

Ranunculus repens
(ruh-**NUNG**-kyoo-lus **REE**-penz)

Common Name	Buttercup
Leaves	Alternate, triangular shaped, 3 lobed, long petioles
Flowers	Yellow, small, 5 petals, multiple flowers per stem
Bloom Time	Early summer
Size/Shape	18 inches tall, spreading fast by stolons
Special Requirements	Full sun to part shade and moist soils
Garden Use	Perennial border, groundcover, can be invasive in wet soils
Hardiness Zone	3-6
Other Notes	'Flore Pleno' has double flowers
Your Own Notes	_____
	_____
	_____

Rodgersia pinnata

Rodgersia pinnata
(rod-JUR-see-uh pin-NAY-tuh)

Common Name Featherleaf Rodgersia
Leaves Alternate, pinnate compound with 5-7 leaflets, bronze in spring
Flowers Pink, very small, in terminal panicles
Bloom Time Late spring to midsummer
Size/Shape 3-4 feet tall, 4 feet wide
Special Requirements Full sun to part shade, moist soils
Garden Use Near ponds, shade garden with moist soils
Hardiness Zone 5-7
Other Notes *Rodgersia aesculifolia* has palmate leaves (lower right) and white flowers
Your Own Notes _____

Rudbeckia fulgida

Rudbeckia fulgida
(rud-BEK-ee-uh FUL-jih-duh)

Common Name	Black-Eyed Susan; Orange Coneflower
Leaves	Alternate, oblong, slightly hairy, dark green
Flowers	Gold rays, brown disk flowers, long lasting, deadhead for rebloom
Bloom Time	Midsummer to fall
Size/Shape	18 to 30 inches tall, 24 inches wide
Special Requirements	Full sun to part shade, good drainage
Garden Use	Perennial border, group, mass
Hardiness Zone	3-8
Other Notes	Var. *sullivantii* 'Goldsturm' is a popular cultivar (pictured lower right)
Your Own Notes	_____

Salvia x superba (x sylvestris)

Salvia x superba (x sylvestris)
(SAL-vee-uh syoo-PUR-buh) [sil-VESS-triss]

Common Name	Perennial Salvia
Leaves	Opposite, long and narrow (lanceolate), rough, square stems
Flowers	Blue-purple, small, two-lipped, in dense spikes, square stems
Bloom Time	Early summer
Size/Shape	2-3 feet tall, 24 inches wide
Special Requirements	Full sun, good drainage, moist, deadhead for rebloom
Garden Use	Perennial border, groups
Hardiness Zone	3-8
Other Notes	'May Night' is a compact hybrid with larger flowers, attracts butterflies
Your Own Notes	_____
	_____
	_____

Saponaria ocymoides
(sap-o-NAY-ree-uh o-see-MOY-deez)

Common Name	Rock Soapwort
Leaves	Opposite, ovate, short petiole or sessile, stems are reddish, evergreen
Flowers	Pink, 5 petals, calyx below the flower is cylindrical
Bloom Time	Late spring
Size/Shape	4-10 inches tall, trailing
Special Requirements	Full sun, good drainage, avoid clay soils
Garden Use	Rock gardens, raised beds, stone walls
Hardiness Zone	3-7
Other Notes	
Your Own Notes	_____
	_____
	_____

Saponaria officinalis

Saponaria officinalis
(sap-o-NAY-ree-uh o-fiss-ih-NAY-liss)

Common Name	Bouncing Bet, Soapwort
Leaves	Opposite, simple, ellipitical, 2-4 inches long, dark green
Flowers	Pink, 5 notched petals, terminal clusters, fragrant
Bloom Time	Midsummer
Size/Shape	12-30 inches tall, 18 inches wide, spreading by stolons
Special Requirements	Full sun to part shade, good drainage
Garden Use	Perennial border, mass, natural areas
Hardiness Zone	2-8
Other Notes	'Rosea-plena' has double flowers and is a popular cultivar
Your Own Notes	_____

Scabiosa caucasica

Scabiosa caucasica
(skay-bee-O-suh kaw-KASS-ih-kuh)

Common Name Pincushion Flower
Leaves Opposite, narrow basal leaves and lobed stem leaves
Flowers Light blue, outer ring of flat petals, center has smaller petals
Bloom Time Summer
Size/Shape 18-24 inches tall, 18 inches wide
Special Requirements Full sun, good drainage, mulch, deadhead, avoid clay soils
Garden Use Groups of 3 for best effect, butterfly gardens
Hardiness Zone 3-7
Other Notes 'Butterfly Blue' is a popular cultivar
Your Own Notes _____
_____
_____

Sedum x 'Autumn Joy' ('Herbstfreude')

Sedum x 'Autumn Joy' ('Herbstfreude')
(SEE-dum)

Common Name	Autumn Joy Sedum
Leaves	Opposite, thick fleshy leaves, toothed
Flowers	Dark pink, small, in terminal clusters
Bloom Time	Late summer into fall
Size/Shape	18-24 inches tall, 15 inches wide, round habit
Special Requirements	Sun to part shade, good drainage
Garden Use	Edge of border, rock garden, group, mass
Hardiness Zone	3-10
Other Notes	'The Clown' (picture on the lower right) has variegated foliage
Your Own Notes	_____
	_____
	_____

Sempervivum tectorum

Sempervivum tectorum
(sem-pur-VY-vum tek-TOH-rum)

Common Name Hen and Chicks
Leaves Alternate, oblong, thick and fleshy, attached at the crown, grow in a rosette, evergreen
Flowers Purple-red, small, in a flat cluster, on a hairy stem
Bloom Time Midsummer
Size/Shape 3-4 inches tall, 3-4 inches wide
Special Requirements Full sun and very good drainage (sand and gravel)
Garden Use Rock gardens, stone walls
Hardiness Zone 3-8
Other Notes
Your Own Notes _____
_____
_____

Solidago hybrids

Solidago hybrids
(sol-ih-**DAY**-go)

Common Name Goldenrod
Leaves Alternate, 2-5 inches long, lanceolate, rough, serrate margins
Flowers Bright yellow, small, in branched panicles
Bloom Time Late summer
Size/Shape 2-3 feet tall, 18 inches wide
Special Requirements Full sun to part shade, good drainage, attracts butterflies
Garden Use Perennial border
Hardiness Zone 2-8
Other Notes 'Fireworks' is a popular cultivar with a compact habit and larger flowers
Your Own Notes _____
_____
_____

Stachys byzantina

Stachys byzantina
(STAY-kiss by-zan-TY-nuh)

Common Name Lamb's Ears
Leaves Gray-green to silver in color, soft hairs, oblong, entire margin, square stems
Flowers Purplish-pink, small, on 4-6 inch spikes
Bloom Time Midsummer
Size/Shape 12-15 inches tall, 18 inches wide, spread by creeping stems
Special Requirements Full sun, good drainage, dry soils
Garden Use Edging, groundcover
Hardiness Zone 4-8
Other Notes Can be invasive
Your Own Notes _____
_____
_____

Stachys macrantha (grandiflora)

Stachys macrantha (grandiflora)
(STAY-kiss muh-KRAN-thuh) [gran-dih-FLOR-uh]

Common Name	Big Betony
Leaves	Ovate, dark green, wrinkled, rough, square stems
Flowers	Violet purple, 2-lipped, on 12 inch tall spikes
Bloom Time	Late spring to early summer
Size/Shape	18 inches tall 12 inches wide
Special Requirements	Full sun to part shade, good drainage
Garden Use	Perennial border, groups
Hardiness Zone	3-8
Other Notes	
Your Own Notes	_____
	_____
	_____

Stachys officinalis

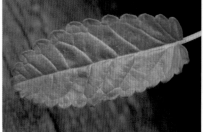

Stachys officinalis
(STAY-kiss o-fiss-ih-NAY-liss)

Common Name	Wood Betony, Bishop's Wort
Leaves	Ovate, 4-5 inches long, large rounded teeth, long petioles
Flowers	Violet-pink, 15-20 flowers in a spike above the leaves
Bloom Time	Late spring
Size/Shape	18-24 inches tall, 24 inches wide
Special Requirements	Full sun to part shade, good drainage
Garden Use	Perennial border, groups
Hardiness Zone	4-8
Other Notes	
Your Own Notes	_____
	_____
	_____
	_____

Tanacetum parthenium

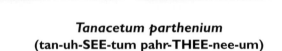

Tanacetum parthenium
(tan-uh-SEE-tum pahr-THEE-nee-um)

Common Name	Feverfew, Matricaria; Chamomile
Leaves	Alternate, pinnate lobes, deeply cut, fern-like, fragrant when crushed
Flowers	White rays, creamy disk flowers, small, in clusters
Bloom Time	Mid to late summer
Size/Shape	1-3 feet tall, 2 feet wide
Special Requirements	Full sun to part shade, good drainage, self-seeds
Garden Use	Perennial border
Hardiness Zone	5-8
Other Notes	'Flore Pleno' has double flowers
Your Own Notes	_____
	_____
	_____

Thalictrum aquilegifolium

Thalictrum aquilegifolium
(thuh-LIK-trum ak-wih-LEE-jih-FO-lee-um)

Common Name Columbine Meadow Rue
Leaves Alternate, bipinnate compound, gray-green, looks similar to columbine leaves
Flowers Pink to lilac, small, in clusters, fluffy appearance
Bloom Time Late spring
Size/Shape 2-3 feet tall, 3 feet wide
Special Requirements Full sun to part shade, good drainage, moist soils
Garden Use Perennial border, wildflower garden
Hardiness Zone 5-8
Other Notes
Your Own Notes _____
_____
_____

Tiarella cordifolia

Tiarella cordifolia
(ty-uh-REL-uh; tee-uh-REL-uh kor-dih-FO-lee-uh)

Common Name	Foam Flower
Leaves	Basal, heart shaped, 3-5 lobes, reddish veins
Flowers	White, small, in 6-9 inch racemes
Bloom Time	Midspring
Size/Shape	6-12 inches tall, spreads to 24 inches
Special Requirements	Part to full shade, good drainage, moist
Garden Use	Shade garden, mass
Hardiness Zone	3-8
Other Notes	
Your Own Notes	_____

_____
_____

Tradescantia virginiana

Tradescantia virginiana
(trad-ess-KAN-she-uh vur-jin-ee-AY-nuh)

Common Name	Spiderwort
Leaves	Alternate, grass-like, 15 inches long, 1 inch wide
Flowers	Violet-purple, white, pink, red, 3 petals, in terminal clusters, each flower lasts one day
Bloom Time	Late spring to midsummer
Size/Shape	18-24 inches tall, 24 inches wide
Special Requirements	Full sun to part shade, moist to wet soils
Garden Use	Border, natural areas, bog garden
Hardiness Zone	3-9
Other Notes	Many cultivars with different colored flowers
Your Own Notes	_____
	_____
	_____

Tricyrtis hirta

Tricyrtis hirta
(try-SUR-tiss HUR-tuh)

Common Name	Toad Lily
Leaves	Alternate, ovate, parallel veins, wrap around the stem, hairy
Flowers	Light purple with dark purple spots, small, in the axils of the leaves, 1-3 together
Bloom Time	Late summer to early fall
Size/Shape	2-3 feet tall and arching, 2 feet wide, no spreading by suckers
Special Requirements	Part shade, moist soils
Garden Use	Shade garden
Hardiness Zone	4-8
Other Notes	*Tricyrtis formosana* (pictured lower left and right) spreading by suckers and flowering at the terminals
Your Own Notes	_____
	_____
	_____

Trollius chinensis (ledebourii)

Trollius chinensis (ledebourii)
(TROL-ee-us chin-EN-siss) [leh-dih-BOR-ee-eye]

Common Name	Chinese Globeflower
Leaves	Deeply cut lobed leaves
Flowers	Golden yellow, cupped petals surround narrow upright petals and stamens
Bloom Time	Early summer
Size/Shape	2-3 feet tall, 30 inches wide
Special Requirements	Full sun to part shade, moist soils
Garden Use	Wet areas in a perennial border, near ponds
Hardiness Zone	3-6
Other Notes	
Your Own Notes	_____

Verbascum chaixii

Verbascum chaixii
(vur-BASS-kum key-IX-ee-eye; kee-ICKS-ee-eye)

Common Name	Nettle-leaved Mullein
Leaves	Alternate, 6 inches long, gray-green, hairy, rounded teeth on the margin
Flowers	White, purple stamens create an "eye," 1 inch flowers on terminal racemes
Bloom Time	Early summer
Size/Shape	3 feet tall, 18-24 inches wide
Special Requirements	Full sun to part shade, good drainage, avoid wet soils
Garden Use	Groups, perennial border
Hardiness Zone	5-8
Other Notes	'Southern Charm' is a hybrid with pink flowers (lower picture)
Your Own Notes	_____
	_____
	_____

Veronica longifolia

Veronica longifolia
(vur-ON-ih-kuh long-ih-FO-lee-uh)

Common Name	Long-leaf Speedwell
Leaves	Opposite to whorled, 2-4 inches long, sharp teeth, slightly hairy, round stems
Flowers	Lilac, small, in 12 inch long racemes
Bloom Time	Summer 6-8 weeks
Size/Shape	24-48 inches tall, 24 inches wide
Special Requirements	Full sun to part shade, moist soils, deadhead for rebloom
Garden Use	Perennial border, groups
Hardiness Zone	4-8
Other Notes	'Blue Giant' is a cultivar with lavender-blue flowers (picture on top)
Your Own Notes	_____
	_____
	_____

Veronica spicata

Veronica spicata
(vur-ON-ih-kuh spy-KAY-tuh)

Common Name	Spiked Speedwell
Leaves	Opposite, lanceolate, 2 inches long, rounded teeth on the margin
Flowers	Blue, on dense spikes, round stems
Bloom Time	Late spring to midsummer
Size/Shape	10-36 inches tall (depends upon cultivar), 24 inches wide
Special Requirements	Full sun to part shade, good drainage, attracts butterflies
Garden Use	Perennial border
Hardiness Zone	3-8
Other Notes	'Goodness Grows' and 'Sunny Border Blue' are very popular hybrids
Your Own Notes	_____
	_____
	_____

Index by Binomial Name

Index by Common Name

a